With the great sense of an experienced researcher and educator, Jen Katz-Buonincontro leads us through the "why" and "how" of qualitative research practices, from reflecting and deciding upon theoretical perspectives and research design, to the nuts-and-bolts of crafting interview protocols, coding, analyzing, and presenting rich qualitative data. Written with candor and in a conversational tone, the book emphasizes the role of reflexivity and positionality in building respectful relationships between researchers and interviewees, an ingredient that ultimately leads to uncovering and telling delightful truths about people and their experiences. This comprehensive guide to interviewing and conducting focus groups, full of useful tips and resources, is a must-have for new and seasoned qualitative researchers alike.

—**Magdalena G. Grohman, PhD,** Associate Director and Researcher at Center for Values
  in Medicine, Science, and Technology, The University of Texas at Dallas

I highly recommend *How to Interview and Conduct Focus Groups* to university instructors who are teaching interview methods and to students who are learning them. Katz-Buonincontro describes key differences between one-on-one interviews and focus group interviews and provides detailed strategies for conducting interviews, transcribing them, and coding and analyzing interview data. She also explains the key roles of theory and researcher identity in the research process and how to prepare one's qualitative results for publication. This will be a very useful guide for novice researchers!

—**Peter Youngs, PhD,** Professor, Department of Curriculum, Instruction, and Special
  Education, University of Virginia, Charlottesville

How to Interview and Conduct Focus Groups

Concise Guides to Conducting Behavioral, Health, and Social Science Research Series

Conducting Your Literature Review
  Susanne Hempel

Designing and Proposing Your Research Project
  Jennifer Brown Urban and Bradley Matheus van Eeden-Moorefield

How to Interview and Conduct Focus Groups
  Jen Katz-Buonincontro

Managing Your Research Data and Documentation
  Kathy R. Berenson

Selecting and Describing Your Research Instruments
  Kelly S. McClure

Writing Your Psychology Research Paper
  Scott A. Baldwin

How to Interview and Conduct Focus Groups

JEN KATZ-BUONINCONTRO

CONCISE GUIDES TO CONDUCTING BEHAVIORAL, HEALTH, AND SOCIAL SCIENCE RESEARCH

 AMERICAN PSYCHOLOGICAL ASSOCIATION

Published by
American Psychological Association
750 First Street, NE
Washington, DC 20002
https://www.apa.org

Order Department
https://www.apa.org/pubs/books
order@apa.org

In the U.K., Europe, Africa, and the Middle East, copies may be ordered from Eurospan
https://www.eurospanbookstore.com/apa
info@eurospangroup.com

Typeset in Minion by Circle Graphics, Inc., Reisterstown, MD

Printer: Gasch Printing, Odenton, MD
Cover Designer: Naylor Design, Washington, DC

Library of Congress Cataloging-in-Publication Data

Names: Katz-Buonincontro, Jen, author.
Title: How to interview and conduct focus groups / by Jen Katz-Buonincontro.
Description: Washington, DC : American Psychological Association, [2022] |
    Series: Concise guides to conducting behavioral, health, and social
    science research series | Includes bibliographical references and index.
Identifiers: LCCN 2021062839 (print) | LCCN 2021062840 (ebook) |
    ISBN 9781433833793 (paperback) | ISBN 9781433839306 (ebook)
Subjects: LCSH: Focus groups. | Social sciences--Research--Methodology. |
    Interviewing in sociology. | BISAC: PSYCHOLOGY / Research & Methodology |
    SOCIAL SCIENCE / Research
Classification: LCC H61.28 .K38 2022 (print) | LCC H61.28 (ebook) |
    DDC 001.4/33--dc23/eng/20220113
LC record available at https://lccn.loc.gov/2021062839
LC ebook record available at https://lccn.loc.gov/2021062840

https://doi.org/10.1037/0000299-000

Printed in the United States of America

10 9 8 7 6 5 4 3 2 1

Dedicated to my dear father, David Michael Katz,
a warm and loving supporter of all my interests and endeavors,
no matter how small.

Contents

CONTENTS

Series Foreword

Why are you reading this book? Perhaps you have recently been assigned to write a research paper in an undergraduate course. Maybe you are considering graduate school in one of the behavioral, health, or social science disciplines, such as psychology, public health, nursing, or medicine, and know that having a strong research background gives you a major advantage in getting accepted. Maybe you simply want to know how to conduct research in these areas. Or perhaps you are interested in actually conducting your own study. Regardless of the reason, you are probably wondering—how do I start?

Conducting research can be analogous to cooking a meal for several people. Doing so involves planning (e.g., developing a menu), having adequate resources (e.g., having the correct pots, pans, carving knives, plates), knowing what the correct ingredients are (e.g., what spices are needed), properly cooking the meal (e.g., grilling vs. baking, knowing how long it takes to cook), adequately presenting the food (e.g., making the meal look appetizing), and so forth. Conducting research also involves planning, proper execution, having adequate resources, and presenting one's project in a meaningful manner. Both activities also involve creativity, persistence, caring, and ethical behavior. But just like cooking a meal for several people, conducting research should follow one of my favorite pieces of advice: "Remember that the devil is in the details." If you want your dinner guests to find your meal tasty, you need to follow a recipe properly and measure the ingredients accurately (e.g., too much or little of some of the ingredients can make the entrée taste awful). Similarly, conducting research without properly paying attention to details can lead to erroneous results.

Okay, but what about your question—"How do I start?" This American Psychological Association book series provides detailed but user-friendly guides for conducting research in the behavioral, health, and social sciences from start to finish. I cannot help but think of another food analogy here—that is, the series will focus on everything from "soup to nuts." These short, practical books will guide the student/researcher through each stage of the process of developing, conducting, writing, and presenting a research project. Each book will focus on a single aspect of research, for example, choosing a research topic, following ethical guidelines when conducting research with humans, using appropriate statistical tools to analyze your data, and deciding which measures to use in your project. Each volume in this series will help you attend to the details of a specific activity. All volumes will help you complete important tasks and will include illustrative examples. Although the theory and conceptualization behind each activity is important to know, these books will focus in particular on the how-to of conducting research so that you, the research student, can successfully carry out a meaningful research project.

This volume, by Jen Katz-Buonincontro, focuses on learning how to effectively conduct interviews and focus groups as well as interpreting the findings in a meaningful and valid manner. Such activities can be classified under the umbrella of *qualitative research methods*, a growing area in psychology. Dr. Katz-Buonincontro first introduces us to this field as background. Of greatest aid are the specific steps she delineates concerning the how-to of conducting quality interviews and focus groups. In addition, she provides useful examples of how to combine these activities within a single study as well as how to combine these qualitative strategies with more traditional quantitative methodologies (referred to as *mixed-methods* approaches). Not only do you learn how to conduct interviews and focus groups, but Dr. Katz-Buonincontro also does a superb job of teaching you how to analyze the results of these activities, as well as how to write up your findings. Going back to my cooking analogy, this entire volume provides for a detailed recipe that ultimately leads to a "gourmet" study.

So, the answer to the question "How do I start?" is simple: *Just turn the page and begin reading!*

Best of luck!

—Arthur M. Nezu, PhD, DHL, ABPP
Series Editor

How to Interview and Conduct Focus Groups

Introduction

Welcome to *How to Interview and Conduct Focus Groups*! Are you considering interviews or focus groups as part of your research project? If so, this book is for you. In it, I aim to help people at various stages of their research career. Perhaps this is your first qualitative research project, or you are designing a new mixed-methods research project that will integrate interviews and focus groups into a study that includes quantitative data. Perhaps you already have experience conducting interviews but not focus groups, or vice versa. Whichever project you are working on, this book will help you design, conduct, code, analyze, write up, and publish interview and focus group data. I'll walk you through steps designed to problem-solve areas where you might feel stuck.

How to Interview and Conduct Focus Groups was born out of the need for a concise guide in the core areas of interviewing and conducting focus groups. After teaching in the field of qualitative research methods for many

https://doi.org/10.1037/0000299-001
How to Interview and Conduct Focus Groups, by J. Katz-Buonincontro

years, as well as taking classes and attending seminars and workshops, I have found that people want to be able to pick up these skills quickly. Even though I've conducted qualitative, mixed-methods, and art-based studies that include interviews or focus groups, I constantly reference and consult resources so I don't accidentally skip important details and so I can reread exemplar studies—ones that are systematic and anchored in a clearly articulated methods design. Although many qualitative research books are available, many do not distill the essence of conducting interviews and focus groups. In today's world, people want to learn methods *fast*, yet good interviewing and focus group methods need to meet the standards conveyed in the core traditions within qualitative methods. That's where this book comes in!

This book strikes a balance between describing the how-to steps and situating them within the core qualitative traditions and theories. Because it is a concise guide, the information presented herein is provided in a compact manner meant to complement lengthier textbooks and specialized handbooks. As such, the book is not exhaustive; it does not include the in-depth explanations of theories and seminal methodologists found in other books. The information herein does not override the knowledge provided by methodologists in this area who have more experience than I. Neither is this book meant to be absolute or authoritative. Many researchers would contest the idea that there's only one way to do qualitative research, but it is my aim to provide clear, essential steps to build your knowledge and skills. The steps I describe in each chapter are intended to guide novice researchers, but experienced researchers may wish to adapt them according to their personal preference or use them to guide their instruction of students or trainees. Three aims guide this book:

- to answer questions you have about when and how to use the methods described,
- to dispel your doubts about how to combine data to meet standards of validity and reliability, and
- to help you break through problems you might encounter along the way.

Chapter 1 provides an overview of the importance of interviews and focus groups, as well as qualitative research designs, skills, and methods.

I describe how qualitative research designs emerged from social theories (e.g., feminism, social interactionism, critical theory) and paradigms of social science (positivism, interpretivism). Next, I explain the skill of developing *reflexivity*, or self-awareness, of the interview and focus group process and how it will help you situate your own identity in the context of the research. I then delve deeper into each respective method. I wrote this book with the assumption that you have already identified your research topic and research problem and that you have completed your literature review.[1]

Chapter 2 describes 12 steps that are essential to conducting quality interviews, from aligning the interview questions with the research question to identifying a type of interview and then designing and pilot-testing an interview protocol. Conducting online interviews is also discussed.

Chapter 3 describes eight essential steps to conducting focus groups and explains how they differ from interviews. For example, I show how sampling groups of people for focus groups contrasts with sampling people to interview. I also suggest strategies for using technological aids, managing the dynamics of group process, and honing your facilitation or moderator techniques.

Chapter 4 includes 10 examples of combining interview and focus groups in one study and discusses ways to combine them with quantitative data.

Chapter 5 focuses on the concepts of quality, validity, and reliability when both interview and focus group methods are being used and interpreting the results. It includes 10 steps for ensuring validity and four steps for addressing reliability.

The processes of transcription, including organizing and formatting transcriptions with notations, as well as suggestions for writing memos, are laid out in Chapter 6. Coding methods, coding books, and triangulating coding across team members also are discussed.

Chapter 7 helps orient researchers to diverse qualitative coding methodologies and the various types of software, such as Dedoose (https://www.dedoose.com/) or NVivo (https://www.qsrinternational.com/nvivo-qualitative-data-analysis-software/home), for assisting—but not replacing—the iterative process of coding transcriptions and deriving categories and themes.

---

[1] You may wish to reference other titles in APA's *Concise Guides* series for help or a refresher on these topics.

Finally, Chapter 8 discusses writing and publishing results (also referred to as *findings*). The chapter includes tips for creating figures and tables and consulting the American Psychological Association's (APA's) Journal Article Reporting Standards in Qualitative Research (https://apastyle.apa.org/jars) and the *Publication Manual of the American Psychological Association* (7th ed.; APA, 2020). Seven steps focus on writing up the findings or results using a variety of rhetorical conventions. Six steps describe comprehensive discussion sections, and four steps cover publishing, including how to convert a thesis or dissertation into an article suitable for publication.

The book's Conclusion is a brief chapter that sums up a few reasons why I have made a career in qualitative research. It offers an opening for you to feel inspired and find your own "why."

Last, you will find two appendices. Appendix A is an at-a-glance review of all the action steps described in this book for conducting interviews and focus groups, looking at the data you collect from them, and writing up the project. You can use this appendix as a checklist or just as a quick reference for gauging your progress toward project completion. If you've forgotten how to do a step, you can easily flip back to the right chapter and read the detailed explanation again. Appendix B includes resources to help you further your work as a qualitative researcher. These resources include a list of programs, degrees, and certificates in qualitative research offered by various institutions; a list of qualitative research institutes; and a list of professional associations for qualitative researchers.

My hope is that by the time you finish these pages you'll feel like you can take on a new interview or focus group project. By providing clear steps and examples, I hope this book can help mitigate fears about starting and completing a research project on your own and help you feel confident along the way. The more comfortable you feel doing research, the more practice you'll get, which will lead to new and creative research ideas.

1

Qualitative Research Essentials

Gathering data through interviews and focus groups is an increasingly recognized and valued skill for behavioral, health, and social science researchers. These qualitative methods developed out of the need to systematically and carefully ask questions and record and interpret responses on important topics as part of larger inquiries in the social sciences (psychology, education, anthropology, sociology, political science, economics, and related fields). It is common knowledge that research generally stems from the researcher's own life experience, observations, and thoughts (Baldwin, 2018). Therefore, the power of interviews and focus groups lies in their potential to unlock keys to our lived experiences by unearthing voices of people, some of whom may live in marginalized communities.

https://doi.org/10.1037/0000299-002
How to Interview and Conduct Focus Groups, by J. Katz-Buonincontro
Copyright © 2022 by the American Psychological Association. All rights reserved.

In this chapter, you'll learn about the power of interviews and some key facts about qualitative research. You'll take the first step toward designing your research project by writing your research stance or positionality statement. This reflexive practice will inform your study design and, in turn, your interactions with people.

WHY ARE INTERVIEWS AND FOCUS GROUPS IMPORTANT? A BRIEF HISTORY

Although quantitative research represents the lion's share of methods used in the social sciences, in particular in psychology, its use has risen over the past 60 years. This increase builds on significant periods of growth in qualitative methodology marked by social upheaval (1960s), ideological conflicts (1970s), critical theory and feminism (1980s), participation and action (1990s), and legitimacy and diversification (2000s).

However, interviewing did not start in the 1960s—it has a long history. Evidence suggests that qualitative methods in psychology and other fields incorporated interviewing before it was acknowledged as a formal research method. Early psychological theories and constructs used qualitative research to explore concepts such as race, class, group process, intergroup conflict, living in mental institutions, morality, and self-actualization, for example. Pioneering social scientist W. E. B. Du Bois (1896/1967) designed and executed some of the first large-scale studies, including interviewing African American Philadelphians about their life experience in school, work, and health care. With this research, Du Bois not only promoted an understanding of racially segregated cities and the inadequate resources for African American communities but also challenged scientific racism. Botkin (1945) interviewed formerly enslaved people, yielding critical oral narratives to defy racist interpretations of the American experience that overlooked African American life and historical experiences. These interviews concentrated on the transition from slavery to freedom. Although this body of research has been criticized because it was conducted mostly by White interviewers, it marked a new way of conducting research during the 1930s in that it attempted to provide a voice for, and thereby dignify the stories of, African American former slaves who developed their own cultural autonomy and traditions (Hirsh, 1945). By dignifying people's stories, interview research helps honor lived experiences to create a more inclusive society.

The interview method was also used for other reasons during this time period. For example, sociologist Paul Lazarsfeld (1935) stressed the asking of questions to understand people's motivations. Child psychologist Jean Piaget (1923/1961) developed the "clinical interview" (Duveen, 2000) and interviewed his own children to unpack cognitive processes and developmental stages. In one study, Piaget (1923/1961) recorded 1,125 spontaneous questions asked by a colleague's 6-year-old son to examine underlying patterns of reasoning in the areas of causal explanation, motivation, and justification.

For all the helpful insights it provided, qualitative research in the 1930s suffered from a lack of theory building and an overreliance on description (Glaser & Strauss, 1967). Researchers continued to develop qualitative research methods beyond the use of interviews for description alone. Interviews also emerged as a way to explore and pilot-test questions for surveys and questionnaires. Margaret Mead (1938) and other anthropologists shed light on American life through fieldwork in schools (Waller, 1932), gangs, and other social groups. Building on the interviewing method, Robert Merton developed the basis of focus groups from Lazarsfeld's (1935) group interview technique. In addition, Lawrence Kohlberg (1958) interviewed adolescents about moral dilemmas and then conducted focus groups with them to observe how they might come to a consensus about solving such dilemmas (Wertz et al., 2011). Other fields, such as anthropology, sociology, education, and health sciences, are increasingly using qualitative methods. In this book, you will see how interviews and focus groups have been integrated into a wide range of qualitative designs and how they can be used in conjunction with quantitative data (this is discussed in more detail in Chapter 4).

FEATURES OF QUALITATIVE RESEARCH

What are the key features of qualitative research? Instead of observing people in controlled experimental laboratories, qualitative researchers study people in naturalistic settings. In this way, qualitative research is humanistic, holistic, and interactive. Qualitative researchers use inductive logic, focusing on emergent and iterative data collection (Glaser & Strauss, 1967). *Inductive logic* involves letting research questions, themes, and codes bubble up to the surface as they occur, as opposed to superimposing hypotheses that narrow down the expected causal relationships among variables in a study.

Balancing *subjectivity* (personal influence and interpretation) with *objectivity* (impartiality) is a fine-tuned skill that qualitative researchers learn to finesse during the collection and analysis of data and interpretation of the results. Subjectivity and objectivity are mutual reinforcers that can strengthen the overall quality of research. Articulating one's role in the research, and how it affects those who participate in interviews, reinforces truthfulness and the resulting dependability of the outcomes that will be scrutinized by the larger research community.

EPISTEMOLOGICAL FRAMEWORKS AND THEORIES DRIVING QUALITATIVE RESEARCH

Various philosophical ways of knowing, or epistemological frameworks, inform research and thus shape the purpose of interviews and focus groups. An *epistemological framework* can be defined as the researcher's lens of knowledge through which the world and the act of research are viewed. *Interpretivism* and *positivism* are two types of epistemologies that examine the nature of reality from opposite ends of the spectrum. Interpretivism, sometimes referred to as *relativism*, relies on multiple truths and realities relative to a specific conceptual scheme (Bernstein, 1998). Historicized, temporal, and individual experience and human agency are showcased (Rossman & Rallis, 1998). Qualitative researchers who use interpretivist frameworks do not see one unified reality. Positivism, in contrast, is concerned with a more detached, objective truth that can be described by relying on "observers" (Bernstein, 1998). These two camps of thought, which were developed in relation to each other over time and across several disciplines, appear to be in opposition to each other. Some researchers stand staunchly in one of these camps. Many, however, see the boundaries between positivism and interpretivism as porous. As such, some researchers oscillate between these two paradigms depending on the nature of the research project.

Symbolic interactionism (Blumer, 1969) is a central theory undergirding qualitative research. It focuses on interpretivism and how people perceive, view, and communicate aspects of their worlds (Dewey, 1930; Mead, 1938). In other words, people see the world in different ways. They also interpret mutual experiences in ways that differ from each other. Symbols used in language are key. These symbols create meaning, and this meaning drives intrapersonal and interpersonal communication as well as social processes and group interactions (Berg, 2004). As you can see, the theory of symbolic interactionism is especially important for interpreting data from interviews and focus groups in which people describe their experience and ascribe meaning to them.

Constructivism relates to symbolic interactionism because it posits that meanings are coconstructed. This implies that reality lies in the interaction between people and is therefore derived from multiple truths.

Phenomenology is another theory that influences the development of qualitative research. It focuses on lived experience (Merleau-Ponty, 1945/1998). Multiple interviews can help unpack the complexity of these experiences.

Critical and *postmodern* epistemological frameworks, including feminism, critical theory, queer theory, intersectionality, and social justice theories (e.g., concerned with goals of liberation and antiracism), push the boundaries of interpretivism even further, to focus on oppression as an inherent element of society, social institutions, and human relationships. Feminism focuses on how gender, patriarchy, and sexism limit both men and women and encompasses African American, Latina, Asian, and White experiences (Tisdell, 2008). Accordingly, a key feature of feminist qualitative research is participation on the part of the study participant in cocreating interview or focus group questions and sometimes publications. Gender and race are highlighted in major theoretical advancements, such as gender-related morality (Gilligan, 1982) and the ethics of care (Noddings, 1984), for example. Each of these epistemological frameworks influences the purpose, direction, and nature of the interview or focus group design and data collection process.

FIVE COMMONLY USED QUALITATIVE RESEARCH DESIGNS

In addition to an epistemological framework, theory is used to select a qualitative or mixed-methods design for research, which in turn shapes the nature of questions to be asked in an interview or a focus group. If a researcher selects *self-efficacy theory* (Bandura, 1997), for example, then they might choose a design with a grounded theory focus that emphasizes the chain of self-determined beliefs that affect learning. As a result, the interview questions might be concerned with the extent to which the interviewee sees their own abilities and how those perceptions and beliefs might shape or trigger decisions, choices, and even behaviors.

Qualitative research designs typically, though not always, adopt one of five foci: (a) ethnography, (b) narrative research, (c) phenomenology, (d) grounded theory, and (e) case study. These are described in the sections that follow and summarized in Table 1.1.

Ethnography: Illuminating Culture

An interview or focus group with a cultural focus, also known as an *ethnography* design (Adler & Adler, 1998; Van Maanen, 1998; Wolcott, 1999), examines patterns of shared beliefs and identities on the basis of group affiliations, histories, and backgrounds. Cultural anthropology, sociology, and education are the core fields that use ethnography. *Emic*, or insider, views of groups of people are considered most valuable. Although participant observation is a core method of this focus, interviews play an important data collection role. Critical ethnography further focuses on social injustices as part of individual and collective experience.

Table 1.1

Types of Interview and Focus Group Data

Type of data	Dimension				
	Person-level focus	Primary purpose	Type of qualitative design and focus	Duration	Common uses with other types of data
Individual interview	Individuals	In-depth description and disclosure of perspectives, beliefs, experiences, etc., that can be confidential	■ Basic design ■ Ethnography (culture) ■ Narrative (life story) ■ Phenomenology (lived experience) ■ Grounded theory (processes and conditions) ■ Case study (contextualize and triangulate data)	30 minutes–1 hour Can be held multiple times	Can stand alone or complement a survey, observations, or other data
Dyadic or small-group interview	Children, young persons	Information that can be better obtained through the comfort of being with another person		20–30 minutes or more	
Structured focus group	Existing groups (e.g., members of a class)	Group experience interactions	■ Evaluation of programs (used more with focus groups)	45 minutes–1 hour	Used to develop items on a survey

Narrative: Telling Life Stories

A project with a *narrative* design (Angrosino, 1989; Clandinin, 2007; Czarniawska, 2004; Polkinghorne, 1988) looks at in-depth narratives, or stories. In contrast to ethnography, narrative designs trade breadth for depth. The autobiographical material gathered through interviewing uses core metaphors to organize anecdotal descriptions of one person. These anchoring metaphors explore complex phenomena, personal history, and how the individual relates to a larger social world (Angrosino, 1989).

Phenomenology: Describing Lived Experience

Phenomenology designs (e.g., Colaizzi, 1978; Moustakas, 1994) highlight the dimensions of experiencing a certain phenomenon through successive, multiple interviews with the same participant or set of participants over time. *Cognitive representations* (Anderson & Spencer, 2002) of individuals describe their idiosyncratic thoughts; emotional responses; and other experiences, such as coping mechanisms and symptoms with illness. Across interviews, these phenomena are characterized as essential structures to promote empathic understanding.

Grounded Theory: Unearthing Processes and Conditions

Grounded theory designs (Charmaz, 2011; Glazer & Strauss, 1967; Strauss & Corbin, 1990) attempt to build a theory about the stages and phases of how something occurs or unfolds. Instead of hypothesizing about how people function, grounded theory studies "ground" the theory in the data using the authentic voices of many people from interviews, group interviews or focus groups, and observations. As a result, the theory will describe causal conditions, strategies, and consequences.

Case Study: Illustrating Key Contexts

Case study designs (Merriam, 2009; Patton, 2002; Stake, 2000) frame an interview as a complement to an observation, survey, or other type of data about an individual or set of cases that have commonalities. Multiple sources of data are used in case study designs. Each case is bounded by specific *actors*, or participants in the study. There is a variety of case study types, including intrinsic, instrumental, exploratory, or explanatory. Multiple case studies span similarly bounded, or defined, units to examine similarities and differences. I discuss this in more detail in Chapter 7.

Some qualitative researchers also use what is referred to as a *basic qualitative design* (Merriam, 2009), which does not does not have a singular focus like the designs above. It is possible to combine elements of the designs above or create new terms to describe their studies. For example, autoethnography combines autobiography with ethnography. Critical participatory action research combines critical theory with action research. Throughout this book, I provide brief examples from each of the five qualitative designs just described. Because of space and copyright limitations, I have not provided sample papers illustrating each one; however, in Chapter 8, I include a list of journals that publish exclusively qualitative research. These are an excellent resource for exemplar studies and gaining familiarity with how different research designs work in practice.

GETTING READY TO CONDUCT INTERVIEWS AND FOCUS GROUPS

How do you get ready to interview and conduct focus groups? In addition to selecting a theory and a research design, preparing to interact with people is important. The art of developing reflexivity is the key to the preparation, success, and enjoyment of research. When trying out a new research method, you might not take to it right away. Trying out a new method—sometimes several times—will help you find out what speaks to you or, conversely, what methods do not align well with your values and interests. Over time, you will feel more and more prepared to go "into the field," which is the way social scientists refer to the process of interacting with other people, organizations, and places as part of a study.

In the next section, I describe how my own first interview experience helped me take my first steps toward developing reflexivity and positionality. *Reflexivity* is the process of reflecting on and clarifying your personal drive for doing research and how you, the researcher, will likely influence the research project (see Luttrell, 2010). *Positionality*, which I discuss a bit later in this chapter, refers to the way a researcher positions oneself and one's identity vis-à-vis the people involved in an interview or focus group session (Tisdell, 2008). Oftentimes we assume these processes occur automatically when we complete an assignment in a research course, but I hope the lesson you'll take from my story is that they don't. I recommend writing down reflexive statements and positionality statements and revising them as needed, if for no other reason than to help yourself stay focused and self-aware. These statements can be written after data are collected for the first time or before one enters the field.

When we interview people or moderate a focus group, issues of subjectivity and bias often arise. Therefore, one of the key skills to develop as a qualitative researcher is reflexivity, the process of building self-awareness of one's identity and assumptions as a researcher (Rossman & Rallis, 1998). Reflexivity lies at the core of interviews and focus group preparation. You can begin this process by writing a *positionality statement*, also known as a *research stance*.

EXPERIENTIAL RESEARCH STORY

My first memorable interview experience occurred when I was an undergraduate sociology major. I took a class called "The Chicano/a Experience in the United States," taught by a well-known Chicana scholar visiting my college. We were assigned to interview someone about their ethnic identity, record the interview, interpret it, and compare the interview themes with various theories. I had read several sociological theories, but this was my first interview. "Ah-ha," I thought, "Easy-peasy!"; I just so happened to have a friend, Luis (pseudonym), who was "Chicano"—or so I thought.

Excitedly, I contacted Luis, who consented to my request. In the interview, I asked him about being Mexican American. However, he distinctly stated that he was not Mexican American, he was just "American." Even though Luis's parents had immigrated from Mexico to the United States, he resisted the ethnic classification of Mexican American and never used the term "Chicano" in reference to himself. This puzzled me. I was not sure how to account for Luis's rich immigration background and ethnic identity if he did not see himself as Mexican American. When we turned off the recorder, he inquired, "So how do *you* feel about being Jewish?" Luis was seeking fairness through reciprocity in the dialogue. I had never been asked that question, and I appreciated the fact that he cared enough to ask it.

What emerged was a much richer interview than I could have expected because it spanned both of our families' heritages and personal ethnic identities. This conversation would have never taken place if not for the interview. Although we each posed tough questions, the interview process created a calm oasis of isolated time and space to talk. The interview questions, when adapted for a back-and-forth dialogue, allowed us to reflect on who Luis and I were and contest the ways in which identity was superimposed on us while growing up in different communities and geographical regions in the United States. Although the direction of our conversation was unplanned, we made the interview authentic to who we were at that time. This quality of authenticity planted the seeds of appreciation for the interview process that, for me, grew into a love of research.

RESEARCHER IDENTITY

Book knowledge takes us only so far. Experiential knowledge can expose gaps in knowledge and provide an excellent opportunity to develop a researcher identity. In the example I just provided, the gaps in my knowledge were about my friend's Mexican American cultural identity and my own Jewish identity. These gaps, when explored in a superficial way, can lead to essentialism and monocultural views that negate the complexity of cultural identity by fostering the process of "othering" (Levinas, 1972/2006). As a result of the interview, I realized that I had to develop my own awareness as a White Jewish female researcher. Qualitative researchers refer to this process as *reflexivity*. When Luis turned the tables, so to speak, and interviewed me, it challenged the notion of who was in charge: the researcher or the participant? I experienced what it was like hear questions for the first time on a deeply personal topic. That's a common theme in qualitative research: unearthing complex and personal thoughts, feelings, and beliefs in both the interviewee and, oftentimes, the interviewer.

Let's now take a closer look at further defining *reflexivity* and *bias*.

Reflexivity and Bias

In the qualitative research tradition, researchers do not necessarily try to hide their identity in terms of their race, ethnicity, gender, sexuality, or other type of group affiliation (e.g., being a parent, following a particular religion). Instead, they often use their identity as a source for building relational trust. Personal identity affects researcher identity. We are all biased in certain ways. This conception of bias is different from bias as it relates to quantitative behavioral research, where it is considered a problem, for example, when it alters a seemingly natural behavior and requires efforts to avoid affecting participant responses.

Taking some time to consider your identities and group affiliations, and how they are alike and different from those of the people you want to interview for your research, can influence the way you design your research questions, how your interview protocols will affect your interactions with potential interviewees, and how you interpret their responses to shape the results or findings section of a research report.

So, how do interviewers and focus group moderators navigate ways to use their identity and subjectivity to strengthen data collection? For some researchers, whether they are a member of a particular community group in which they are conducting interviews and focus groups does not matter. However, when there is a *perceived match* between the topic they are investigating and their identity, then researcher identity, life experience, and subjectivity do matter. For example, if a student is an actor and conducts a focus group with actors, then the student may draw on their own knowledge of acting during the focus group.

If a researcher is a member of the community in which they are conducting a focus group, for example, then their relationships might be a source of strength, and their identity can provide a way to bond with study participants (see Luttrell, 2010). As a result, the relationship between the focus group moderator and participants can be symbiotic (see Banks, 1998). However, if the interviewer or focus group moderator is not a member of a specific community in which they are conducting research, then they can address their *positionality* directly with participants to clarify and contextualize their relationship. Let's dig deeper into positionality.

Positionality

Positionality statements can be included in research assignments, papers, theses and dissertations, grant applications, tenure and promotion dossiers, leadership statements, and other incidences where disclosing one's identity and stance helps inform the quality of the research process and outcomes. Every time you write, you create a relationship with the reader; as such, positionality statements help you build a relationship with the people who are your study participants as well as your audience. An aim of these statements is to build trust in an authentic manner between the researcher and the community with whom they intend to engage.

Positionality statements fall on a continuum of phrasing, ranging from mild disclaimers, such as a research stance, to statements acknowledging imbalances in power between the researcher and the people participating in the research study.

For example, Esposito et al. (2019; see Exhibit 1.1) first disclosed their racial identity as "White" and national identity as "Europeans." They acknowledged the privilege affiliated with their university status and socioeconomic class. This acknowledgment helps call attention to an imbalance of power, wherein those in academia are considered to hold a dominant social status in society. Instead of assuming that people won't see or experience that imbalance, the researchers chose to describe it in an explicit statement. In their study, they interviewed people who were detained in immigration facilities because of their perceived illegal status. With candor, Esposito et al. described the distrust between researcher and

Exhibit 1.1

Positionality Statement

Through such critical engagement we also aimed to reposition the power granted to us as White Europeans with university affiliations via passionate solidarity and informed empathy with protagonists struggling "from the margins" (Lykes, 2013). Particularly, we tried to put our privilege to work in the service of detainees by sharing the information that we had access to with them (i.e., concerning rights, laws, procedures, and sources of support and information available inside Ponte Galeria), as well as by supporting them, at least emotionally, in their struggles. Furthermore, and in alignment with critical ethnography's commitment to a "decolonizing standpoint" (Reyes Cruz & Sonn, 2011), we adopted a transdisciplinary attitude in order to unpack and, thus, challenge the micropolitical processes of detention and how the enduring legacy of colonialism, in inter-section with other systems of power, influences such processes. Such a critical engagement, however, was not always straightforward. Our privilege in terms of socioeconomic, educational, and citizenship statuses inevitably challenged the research process and the relation-ships formed with detainees, at times provoking distant, distrustful, or aggressive attitudes toward the study (Esposito, 2019).

Note. From "Ecology of Sites of Confinement: Everyday Life in a Detention Center for Illegalized Non-Citizens," by F. Esposito, J. Ornelas, E. Briozzo, and C. Arcidiacono, 2019, *American Journal of Community Psychology, 63*(1-2), p. 194 (https://doi.org/10.1002/ajcp.12313). Copyright 2019 by Wiley.

participants that can be traced to this imbalance of power. Navigating relationships in research involving people who might have a history of distrust of academics, institutions, government officials, or politicians because of political persecution or historical racism, for example, can be tricky. A positionality statement can help a researcher address the relationship in the short term with research participants and, later, with journal readers.

Steps for Writing a Research Stance or Positionality Statement

Use Exhibit 1.1 as an exemplar positionality statement to accompany these five steps:

1. Think about why you would like to engage in an interview/focus group with a particular person or community.
2. Reflect on your identity as a researcher.
3. Consider how your identity relates to the community in which you will conduct research, including the identity of study participants.
4. Acknowledge dynamics such as marginalization, privilege, and equality in terms of your researcher identity.
5. Elucidate your interests, strengths, and knowledge related to the study.

Writing about your relationship to your research topic and to the communities who will engage in your research is the first core step in interviewing and conducting focus groups.

In Chapter 2, I discuss how you can use this basic skill to build relationships and communication skills with study participants. I list and describe 12 essential interviewing steps. One of these steps involves submitting a human subjects protocol with consent forms to explain to study participants the concepts of voluntary participation, confidentiality, and anonymity. This links back to the idea of sharing power and protecting the rights of study participants introduced in positionality statements. In Chapter 5, I return to positionality as a part of cultivating validity in interviews and focus groups.

2

Interviews

Do you remember the last time you interviewed for a job? Probably! One of the reasons we remember times like this is because it was a personally meaningful, high-stakes experience, perhaps fraught with a feeling of expectation as well as a healthy dose of uncertainty and nerves. If you are new to interviewing, you may find it a bit nerve-racking, and at first it can be, especially if you have not yet met the person face to face. Likewise, the interviewees you question can feel uncertain or on edge. Therefore, trust and psychological safety are paramount to the interview process.

https://doi.org/10.1037/0000299-003
How to Interview and Conduct Focus Groups, by J. Katz-Buonincontro

Interviews are the hallmark of qualitative research (Rossman & Rallis, 1998). Now that you have learned some background information about qualitative research, it is time to leverage those skills to design, plan, and conduct an interview. The 12 steps in this chapter will help you plan and execute successful interviews while keeping respectful relationships and clarity of communication central to the process.

WHY ARE RELATIONSHIP-BUILDING AND COMMUNICATION SKILLS IMPORTANT FOR RESEARCHERS?

Good relationship-building and communication skills are a key part of your research toolkit. These skills come into play even before your first interview with a research participant. You need them when working with a supervising professor, advisor, or the research team executing the project. One tool for building cohesion and trust across the members of the research team is writing and sharing a positionality statement or research stance, which was explored in Chapter 1. As a group activity, this type of exercise not only creates an opportunity to clarify each team member's interest in the project but also allows the team to develop a strong conceptual analysis of the data you anticipate gathering, coding, and writing up (C. A. Barry et al., 1999). If you are working with just one collaborator, such as an advisor, writing a positionality statement or research stance is still helpful.

In addition to discussing research stances and positionality statements, some teams or advisors create statements to discuss authorship roles before the data collection or publishing phase begins (American Psychological Association Science Directorate, 2015). Discussing author roles and author order (i.e., on a journal article) is advisable to allay concerns about publication, especially because students occupy a less powerful position than professors. These discussions will build a foundation for trust and ensure high standards of professionalism.

Professionalism, in turn, sets the tone for conducting interviews or focus groups. Honesty, candor, and clear communication are important for recruiting prospective study participants, handling data ethically, honoring confidentiality and anonymity, and interpreting results in an authentic manner. Body language and professional, work-appropriate attire in the field are important, too, because they signal that you, as the interviewer, take your responsibility seriously. I return to cultivating trust and rapport with interviewees in the discussion of Step 10, later in this chapter.

ESSENTIAL INTERVIEWING STEPS

Teamwork and professionalism help ensure smooth interviewing. In Chapter 1, I described the nature of epistemological frameworks, undergirding theories that inform qualitative research, the primary focus of each major qualitative research design, and constructing positionality statements. At this point, I presume you have already narrowed down your interview topic, situated that topic in the context of a relevant societal problem, and reviewed the literature in your area to identify key gaps in past research. For more on this topic, see Baldwin's (2018) *Writing Your Psychology Research Paper*. The 12 essential interviewing steps discussed in the following sections will help you design effective and strong interviews.

Step 1: Provide a Rationale for Selecting Interview Methods

It is important to think about why you selected interviewing as your data collection method. Speaking with people is one of the best ways to understand the why and how of human experience and perspectives. Other than observing interactions or asking people to write down their thoughts in a diary or questionnaire, directly speaking with people individually or in groups allows access to their opinions, values, implicit beliefs, and perspectives on a set of topics. Qualitative researcher Michael Patton (2002) summed it up well: "We cannot observe feelings, thoughts, and intentions.

We cannot observe behaviors that took place at some previous point in time" (p. 340). This is why interviews are so important.

In addition to accessing cognition, interviews allow people to express emotional qualities of their experiences, whether that experience involves a fond memory or a conflict they had at work, for example. These emotional qualities are challenging to capture in surveys alone. In fact, some researchers might argue that the validity of what people think is better captured through interviews than surveys. Interviews are important because they provide space and time for the interviewee to express their individual opinion and characterize their life in their own unique way. This process can empower the interviewee if they have not had the chance to discuss their experiences. Researchers also choose interviews because of the interpretive nature of the data; that is, qualitative researchers acknowledge the researcher's individualistic approach to interview data collection, which also includes interpretation (Denzin & Lincoln, 2008) in the areas of coding and analysis.

As you work through Step 1, ask yourself:

- How do the interviews relate to my research questions?
- What is the primary rationale for using interview methods as opposed to other types of data collection?

Step 2: Select a Sampling Method

Among the many types of sampling in the social sciences, qualitative research uses *nonprobabilistic sampling strategies* (i.e., whereby participants are purposefully selected because they meet certain criteria), as opposed to the probabilistic random sampling strategies common to quantitative research. *Convenience sampling* refers to recruiting people from an available source of naturally clustered, or grouped, individuals, such as members of a class or classroom, players on a sports team, or members of an organization. *Purposive* (Chein, 1981) or *purposeful* sampling is the technique of sampling according to key characteristics, such a person living with cancer who has a certain background or another "information-rich" attribute

(Patton, 2002). This is also called *criterion-based sampling* (LeCompte & Preissle, 1993).

Maximal variation sampling is designed to represent as diverse as possible set of perspectives from various people on a given subject (Glaser & Strauss, 1967). *Snowball sampling* can be a little more elaborate; the researcher might not know how to contact certain persons or how widespread a group's membership is. In that case, the researcher contacts individuals with a certain characteristic and then asks them to provide information about others who share that same characteristic.

Quota sampling can be used when the researcher aims for a certain number of persons to interview in a category, such as age, gender, ability status, or another characteristic (e.g., reading level). *Community nomination* is another strategy that was developed to select interview participants from a particular community (Foster, 1994); it is also used in domains where experts nominate other experts or in schools where teachers might nominate other teachers or students because they possess outstanding expertise in a certain area (e.g., an award-winning teacher).

Mixed-methods studies can incorporate the above strategies, depending on the type and design of the study. For example, many mixed-methods studies use a two-stage sampling strategy, with Stage 1 as the first data collection method and Stage 2 as the second. If, for example, a population survey with 350 participants is conducted in the first stage of the mixed-methods study, then the researcher might use quota sampling to select a smaller number of participants on the basis of the demographic characteristics of the survey respondents or on the type of responses evidenced in the survey data (e.g., Hattan & Alexander, 2021).

Sample size in qualitative research depends on several factors. One is the degree to which the researcher thinks the topic will be saturated within the specific sample (Lincoln & Guba, 1985). Researchers determine that *saturation* has been achieved when no other data are needed because the research topic has been sufficiently explored by describing the dimensions, conditions, or situations, and therefore the research question has been answered. For example, if you are studying postpartum depression, saturation might be reached when mothers with various types of postpartum depression, social backgrounds, and genetic predispositions have been interviewed to describe a full range of postpartum experiences, and therefore no further interviews are deemed necessary.

Other factors that influence sample size include how many persons are available and willing to participate; whether representativeness has been achieved; or whether the interview data are triangulated with other sources, such as observations and archival data. Resources for conducting the interview, including personnel, time constraints, and participant renumeration, can also affect sample size. Flexibility is key: Sometimes researchers change whom they sample as they collect and analyze data (see Glaser & Strauss, 1967), or they change their sampling tactic depending on the availability of the participants or permission from a research site.

As you work through Step 2, ask yourself:

- What is the best sampling strategy for my interview project?
- What is my sample size, and will I need to make any adjustments?

Step 3: Choose a Qualitative Design and Orientation

In Chapter 1, I provided a simple overview of qualitative research designs. Your next step is to choose a qualitative research design to inform the focus of your interview questions. *Researcher orientations* are the approaches to research they take on the basis of these designs. These orientations have developed over the years. In the following paragraphs, I describe your design options and the researcher orientations that have been honed with each one. Oftentimes it can be hard to decide which design best suits your research project, and you might need to change your design accordingly. Take some time to consider the primary focus of each approach; you might need to change your focus and orientation in the design phase.

Ethnographic interviews (Spradley, 1979) focus on culture situated in the emic, or "insider," perspective of the interviewee. Ethnography involves learning from people, as opposed to studying people (Spradley, 1979). Ethnography recognizes that people live in multiple cultural realities, and, as such, some ethnographers focus on promoting an egalitarian society through activism and anti-racism, for example, that extends beyond the practice of research (Foley & Valenzuela, 2008). Ethnography aims to treat interviewees as empowered collaborators who teach the ethnographer about their cultural experiences. Fittingly, the *orientation* of the ethnographic interviewer is to invoke a state of ignorance—that is, to clear their own mind of preconceptions—and expresses serious interest (Spradley, 1979) so that the interviewees can describe their cultural experiences in their own words to avoid being exoticized. Ethnographic interviewers engage in restating and incorporating key expressions used by the interviewee in the interview—several examples of this are included in Spradley's (1979) book *The Ethnographic Interview*. As a result, a sense of intimate knowledge is generated from interviews that complements data collected during participant observation (Van Maanen, 1982).

Phenomenological interviews focus on the in-depth qualities of a person's lived experience. Attention to temporal or transitory concepts, as well as subjective understandings are garnered through a series of three or more in-depth interviews (Seidman, 2019). Researchers can choose to write about their own experience on the topic or be interviewed by a colleague before interviewing others (Merriam, 2009). Therefore, the orientation of phenomenological interviews is to be open and to reflect on one's own experience in relation to the interviewee's experience. *Phenomenological reduction* is cultivated by exposing the essence of a lived experience. Interviews generate insight into what it is like for people to go through a certain experience (Polkinghorne, 1988).

Narrative interviews, on the other hand, focus more on life history and elicitations of life stories (see Exhibit 2.1). In in-depth narrative interviews, stories are told from the first-person perspective. Various details about the interviewee's biological history, family, and social life, viewed through various disciplinary lenses, are explored in the interviews. Characteristics of narrative interviews include recalling memories, telling stories in your own words, and bearing witness (Botkin, 1945; Reissman, 2008). As such, they are a critical means of conveying authentically one's own stories, as opposed to being misrepresented. The qualities of individuality and transition in one's life are key focal points. Narrative interviewers endeavor to focus on the word choices and phrasing of each spoken act and pay special attention to intonation, pitch, and pauses (Merriam, 2009).

Exhibit 2.1

Example Interview Protocol Using a Narrative Design

Script: Thank you so much for volunteering to participate in this interview. I believe that you are the expert of your own experiences and that only you can tell your story. I appreciate you taking the time to share your insight on homelessness.

Getting Started

- Are you from Chicago/Seattle originally?
  - If yes: What neighborhood are you from? If no: What city/state are you from?

Timeline

- Before we go into more detailed questions, could you give me a brief timeline of your life up to this point?
  - What was a high point in your life? What was a low point in your life?
  - What was a turning point in your life? When things really changed?

Home

- Would you mind if I asked you to tell me a story about your home?
  - What was it like growing up in your home?
- Can you tell me a story that happened to you after leaving home and before coming to live here?

Education

- Can you tell me a story about a positive experience at school?
- Can you tell me a story about a negative experience at school? (Truncated section)

Belonging

- Can you tell me a story about a time that someone hurt your feelings, was not there for you, or did not help you?
- Can you describe a time and place when you felt a sense of belonging?

Exhibit 2.1

Example Interview Protocol Using
a Narrative Design (*Continued*)

Self-Perception

- Can you tell me a story about what your future might look like?
- If you could change three things in your life, what would they be?
  - Do you feel like those things are possible?
- What are three things that you like about yourself or your life?

Ideology

- In your words, what does it mean to be successful? What does it mean to live a good life?
- What does being an American mean to you? How would you describe your religious or spiritual beliefs?

Note. Adapted from "The Lived Experience of Homeless Youth: A Narrative Approach," by E. E. Toolis and P. L. Hammack, 2015, *Qualitative Psychology*, 2(1), pp. 67–68 (https://doi.org/10.1037/qup0000019). Copyright 2015 by the American Psychological Association.

Other types of interviews based on core qualitative designs can be found in the literature (e.g., case studies [Patton, 2002; Stake, 2000; Yin, 2003], grounded theory [Glaser & Strauss, 1967], and action research [Mills, 2000]). Within each design is a specific research topic and set of research questions. Aligning interview questions with research questions prevents the problems of decontextualizing interview results or answering the wrong question (Maxwell, 2005; see Table 2.1). Good interview questions attempt to illuminate and pry open a world of understanding, sometimes taking circuitous routes to do so. As such, interview questions undergo multiple drafts of revision and testing. Interview protocols can be developed through consultation with research advisory boards, community partners, and other stakeholders (see Katz-Wise et al., 2022).

The first step in crafting a good interview protocol is to consult the study's research question and consider the sensitivity of the research topic and any related cultural dimensions. For instance, if you are interviewing

Table 2.1

How to Align Interview Questions and Probes to a Research Topic

Research topic	Sample interview question	Sample interview probe
Gender identity	How do you currently identify your gender?	Do you use different words to identify your gender in different situations or with different people?
Stress and coping	What, if anything, causes you stress related to your gender identity?	Can you give an example of a stressful situation that you faced recently related to your gender identity?

Note. Data from Katz-Wise et al. (2022).

adolescents about their substance abuse, you might first want to interview them about their substance use. To get data about their substance use, you might first want to interview them about what they do during their free time. To understand what they like to do during their free time, you might want to ask them about whom they hang out with, where they go, whether they are supervised, what they do during family holidays, and so on.

Qualitative research questions are open ended. The answer or response should not be limited to a "yes" or a "no" (closed-ended questions). If the answer must include a singular response to clarify an issue, then you would follow up with additional questions to probe for richer responses. *Question stems*, such as "who," "what," "when," "how," and "why," are the beginning part of the interview question. *Question extensions* are ways to expand what you are trying to ask a person in an interview. They are also referred to as *probes* or *follow-up questions* (see Table 2.2). After an initial interview question has been posed, extensions allow the interviewee a chance to reflect and form a detailed response. In addition to specific question extensions, the interviewer can make statements to generate additional detail, such as "This is so interesting, but I'm not sure I get the entire picture yet. Can you tell me more?" or "Can you provide more detail?" (Rossman & Rallis, 1998). In addition, interviewers can present scenarios to see how an interviewee might explain something in a new or different way, for example, "If you were talking to a parent, what would you say?"

Question stem	Question extensions
Introduction	"Tell me more about that . . ."
	"Explain that a little bit more . . ."
How . . .?	"How do you feel . . ."
	"Reflecting on this experience, how would you . . ."
	"How would you define . . ."
	"Now that you are older, how do you feel about . . ."
	"How do you think . . . things would be different/stay the same if . . ."
	"How did things shift . . ."
	"How were you involved . . ."
	"How does this drawing/photograph represent your thoughts about . . ."
What . . .?	"What do you remember/recall . . ."
	"What would you think/feel/say . . ."
	"What are your thoughts/feelings/reasons/experiences . . ."
	"What key moments . . ."
	"What was happening . . ."
	"What changes . . ."
	"What drives you to/makes you want to . . ."
When . . .?	"When you—, what happened next . . ."
	"When did this experience begin . . ."
Why . . .?	"Why did you . . ."
	"Why would you like to . . ."
Where . . .?	"Where does this experience . . ."
	"Where did this happen . . ."

Table 2.2

Interview Question Stems and Extensions

For Step 3, ask yourself:

- Which qualitative design best informs my interview approach?
- Within the chosen design, how would I characterize my research orientation?
- What qualities will I bring to the interview process to address sensitive topics or cultural issues?

Step 4: Find Published Exemplars of Interview Studies

As you refine your interview focus, look for published exemplars of interview studies. These exemplars should lay out clearly the qualitative research design focus, research topic, interview steps or procedure, interview protocol, coding strategy, and data analysis. If you are exploring a new research design, it is important (and fun!) to compare and contrast different designs. You may wish to collect several articles that have used interviews and organize them according to research type: ethnography, narrative, phenomenology, grounded theory, case study, or other type of design. Space constraints prevent many journals from publishing entire interview protocols; however, dissertations often do include them.

If you are using mixed-methods or arts-based research designs, poke around databases to see if there is an exemplary article that has examined your study's general topic using interviews. It's also helpful to organize the articles according to a continuum of the quality of research design: fair, good, and excellent. You can learn what authors omit in their descriptions (fair articles) as well as what details they provide (good) or how well they use rich description to make the research come alive (excellent).

For Step 4, ask yourself:

- What published articles serve as good models for my interview?
- What are the strengths of these articles?

Step 5: Select an Interview Type

At first, you may not know what type of interview you wish to conduct. There's a continuum of basic interview types that can be tailored even further according to the type of design one selects (e.g., ethnographic, phenomenological). *Structured* or *standardized interviews* are like census interviews in that they follow a rigid, proscribed set of questions that do not use probes to obtain additional information. In essence, the questions are like a survey read aloud to each interviewee. As such, structured interviews do not give the interviewee an opportunity to reflect on, discuss, or embellish their responses.

Semistructured interviews are formal and use a consistent set of questions, or a protocol, with each interviewee. Some interviewers allow for new topics of discussion to emerge and to explore topics in depth. Most researchers choose to use a semistructured interview. The advantage is that they strike a balance between a consistent set of questions and flexibility, so participants can discuss what they think is important. Semistructured interviews appeal to the need to use a core structure in the interview but also allow for creativity on the part of the interviewer.

Unstructured interviews, also called *informal* or *unstandardized interviews,* are quite informal and not used as often as semistructured interview protocols. Predetermined questions are not used (Berg, 2004); instead, serendipity is key (Rossman & Rallis, 1998). Researchers spontaneously develop questions, change the order of the questions, and pose different questions to each interviewee, depending on their role. Unstructured interviews are not used frequently by new researchers or researchers examining new topics.

Dialogic interviews comprise a conversation between researcher and participant that represents a balanced ebb and flow of discussion. There might be a number of interesting topics to discuss, but they do not stem from a structured set of questions as laid out in an interview protocol. They are even more flexible than unstructured interviews.

Photo or *art-elicitation interviews* can fall anywhere on the continuum of unstructured to structured. They integrate photos or artistic processes, such as drawing, into the interview process. One reason for integrating a photo or a drawing is to help the interviewee project their thoughts or feelings onto the image (Katz-Buonincontro & Phillips, 2011). These interviews can also help capture daily life activities by recording them in photos and then providing an opportunity to discuss them in an interview setting (Taylor, 2002). Images can provide documentation of the lives of other family members who may not be able to speak or document their own lives (e.g., an infant, an older person, a person with significant physical disabilities). When interviewing children, visual images can help equalize the researcher–interviewee relationship given that words are the domain of adult language and power (Prosser & Burke, 2008). Drawings can be used to help obtain rich descriptions during an interview. For example, Spradley (1979) asked people to draw a map of the inside of a jail and explain what it was like.

For Step 5, ask yourself:

- What type of interview best suits my study: structured, semistructured, unstructured, dialogic, or photo/art elicitation?
- How might an artifact like a photo, image, map, or work of art enrich the interview?

Step 6: Draft an Interview Protocol

As mentioned, most researchers use a semistructured interview. Crafting a good-quality interview protocol requires iterative writing with multiple drafts. Researchers typically start with an introductory script and then organize the interview into smaller topics (e.g., growing up, learning at home, at school, at work). Once each category of question has been amply developed, you can look back at the initial research questions to make sure they link explicitly to the research questions.

You should then think about what the burning or essential questions are. If you had only half the time you had anticipated, which questions do you feel are the most necessary? Provocative questions that might be considered private or sensitive are usually necessary because the responses cannot be obtained anywhere else (from a memo, a website, an email, a blog, an observation, a survey, etc.).

Ordering the questions will help you organize them to provide good flow. In general, interview protocols begin with lighter questions—about the weather, for example—to help segue into the formal part of the interview.

All interview protocols should introduce a simple description of the study and the interviewer. To promote a feeling of security, they should also orient the interviewee to the overall number of the questions. Interviewees should not feel that they've been thrown a curveball question that has no relation to the research project. Providing clear information to the interviewee about the project before the interview, without disclosing the exact details so that you can get fresh, meaningful, and authentic responses, is a delicate balance.

For Step 6, ask yourself:

- What are the essential questions of the interview protocol?
- What's the best order of the questions?

Step 7: Pilot-Test the Interview Protocol

Pilot-testing interview protocols with another student, colleague, or person who is similar to the target interview group is a great way to grow comfortable with talking to someone and revising the interview protocol draft to ensure a smoother flow of questions. Common pitfalls researchers encounter when developing interview protocols are provided as a checklist in Table 2.3. Consult the checklist after you do a dry run of your first protocol draft. Closed-ended questions require conversion to open-ended questions. Two-tailed questions bundle more than one question together and thus need to be separated. Ambiguous or confusing questions require conceptual clarification and grammatical revision.

Questions that do not have capacity to generate new and authentic insight into a topic will likely result in a boring or off-topic conversation. These questions should be reconsidered. Perhaps you have not been able to get at the heart of a matter, or you've had trouble getting interesting responses that could not be obtained through another form of data. Make sure you order the questions in a logical way that starts with warm-up questions and ends with closing questions and an expression of appreciation of the interviewee's time. As you pilot-test the protocol, make note of the length of the interview to see if the responses match the expected duration of the interview. Last, examine your questions to make sure that they do not coerce or lead the participant to answer in a certain way.

For Step 7, ask yourself:

- Who is a good person to interview as I pilot-test my interview protocol?
- What questions should be included in the interview protocol, and which ones should be changed, deleted, or reordered?

Table 2.3

Pilot-Testing Interview Protocols:
Checklist of Common Pitfalls and Possible Solutions

Area	Common pitfalls	Possible solutions to pitfalls
1	Closed-ended questions?	Convert to open-ended questions
2	Two-tailed question?	Change to single question or break-out into multiple question(s)
3	Ambiguous or confusing?	Clarify meaning
4	Probing for obvious information that can be obtained through other sources?	Refocus and strengthen questions to relate more strongly to the study purpose and research questions
5	Poor internal validity or capacity for new and authentic insight on topic?	Rewrite questions to be more direct and that drive at the heart of the matter
6	Ordered illogically and incoherently?	Reorder to start with warm-up questions, and double check the grammar of each question
7	Insufficient length of time?	Provide sufficient wait time to interviewee; allocate additional follow-up time
8	Leading or coercive questions?	Rewrite to be less coercive and more empowering
9	Compatible tone?	Does the tone of the question match the tone of the response? For example, use "How come . . .?" versus "Why?"

Step 8: Submit a Human Subjects Protocol, Including Consent Forms

Interviews involve people, so they are considered human subjects research. As such, studies involving interview data require an approved *human subjects protocol*: a set of forms and agreements submitted to your institution's institutional review board that confirm your ability to conduct research in an ethical manner as well as provide permission to conduct human subjects research. Once your human subjects protocol is approved, you can proceed to recruit people in your sample to participate in the interview. Before starting each interview, provide the consent form to each person. Consent forms clearly indicate that participation in the research study is voluntary and that people who enroll have the option of ending their participation at a later date. All researchers must complete their institution's required training modules. Sometimes your advisor will need to be listed as the principal investigator on the forms; your name and contact information also must be included.

Confidentiality and anonymity are key concepts in interviewing. *Confidentiality* addresses how a researcher handles and protects the identity of the person being interviewed, including responsibly storing that person's name, student ID number, email, address, and other identifiable information. *Anonymity* refers to a person's identity not being disclosed. The researcher should explain to the institutional review board how they plan to maintain confidentiality—for example, by protecting the data on nontransferable files stored on a password-encrypted computer. Interview data are typically reported anonymously in written results by using a general reference to the group, such as "adolescents," or using a pseudonym—a fake name that represents an interviewee—to refer to the study participants. Some researchers choose to keep the ethnic identity of an interviewee's name to preserve the authenticity of the name (see Katz-Buonincontro et al., 2020).

Transparency and *reciprocity* between the interviewer (researcher) and interviewee (participant) rely on disclosure of the perceived benefits of the research to the people you're interviewing and how the research will be used. Whereas the interviewer's goal might be only to analyze interview data for publication and dissemination, for example, participants might find interviewing to be therapeutic, or they may be able to use the study results for public relations purposes (Rossman & Rallis, 1998). Therefore, the researcher must describe the intended perceived benefits in the consent form to be signed by participants as part of the human subjects protocol application. The researcher also can reiterate the benefits when recruiting and obtaining consent from individuals face to face. These practices help promote trust and establish rapport in the unique relationship of interviewer and interviewee.

For Step 8, ask yourself:

- Does my consent form outline clearly the conditions of study participation?
- What assurances do I give regarding confidentiality and anonymity?

Step 9: Recruit Interviewees and Obtain Consent From Them

After receiving approval of human subjects protocols, researchers can start to plan the process of reaching out and contacting those whom they'd like to interview. Liaising with appropriate professionals can give you access to a particular site or population. Designated vulnerable populations, such as prisoners, minors, pregnant women, or those with intellectual impairment or compromised decision-making abilities, require extra diligence, time, and attention. Family caregivers, such as parents or guardians, may need to be consulted in order to assess the cognitive capacity and willingness of some individuals to participate in interviews.

One such example is conducting interview research with persons with Alzheimer's disease, which requires using a calm voice, refraining from using a condescending tone, allowing extra time for responses, and conducting the interview in a familiar room (Beuscher & Grando, 2009). If an individual cannot physically sign a consent form, then a caregiver can sign as a witness. Alternatively, verbal assent can be used when neither the individual nor a caregiver can sign on their behalf. The concept of research might be too frightening or difficult to comprehend for some people, such as those with cognitive impairment, or their families and caregivers might resist participation in a research study (Nicholson et al., 2013). If individuals with cognitive impairment cannot read consent forms or study descriptions, the researcher will need to read aloud the information and describe the study (Fitzgerald & Withers, 2013). In addition, give people extra time to read over the information and consider participation. If a person chooses not to participate, thank them for their time and move on to other possible participants. It's important to maintain good relationships with people and their communities.

For Step 9, ask yourself:

- How will I recruit participants?
- What, if any, special considerations may be necessary, such as working with caregivers, explaining study participation, allowing for extra time, or working with translators?

Step 10: Cultivate Rapport and Trust During the Interview

The quality of rapport between interviewer and interviewee affects the quality of the interview responses. In this way, qualitative researchers refer to themselves as the "instrument," a twist on the term commonly used in quantitative research when referring to a survey instrument. Qualitative researchers must create conditions of trust and rapport to allow participants to open up and disclose authentic beliefs and feelings while at the same time minimizing risk for psychological (or other types of) harm to the participants. The very nature of interviewing creates a power dynamic (Seidman, 2013) that can be slightly uncomfortable at times. To counter the potential effects of this power differential, interviewers should try to cultivate support and empower participants by allowing them to ask questions and share information.

Comembership in interview research means bonding with the interviewees in a professional manner (Rossman & Rallis, 1998). Being a part of the group to which your interviewee belongs, or having "insider" status, can be helpful, but it is not essential to obtaining robust data. For example, feminist researcher Michele Foster (1994) noted that patterns of speech during interviews affect the overall quality and duration of the interview, such that when women speak together, they take turns and thus support each other in sharing their stories. The process of comembership can help preserve the integrity of the researcher–interviewee relationship. If an interviewer identifying as a man, for example, interviews a person who identifies as a woman, then they do not share the same gendered identity and thus may not experience comembership during the interview process. The male interviewer could choose to acknowledge that he may not have experiences similar to those of the female interviewee and thus invite her to share only what she feels comfortable sharing. Another option to accommodate a lack of comembership would be to ask a female research team member to interview only female interviewees and male interviewers to interview only male interviewees. Situations in which this strategy might be especially helpful include discussions of friendships, relationships, or reproductive health issues.

Positive body language and professional attire are also important for cultivating a sense of trust and building rapport. Although a fancy suit is not necessary for establishing a respectful tone, it is important to dress appropriately without revealing one's body inappropriately. When I was a college intern working with a program that treated emotionally disturbed youth, I remember interviewing a 13-year-old boy. Later, my supervisor took me aside and complimented my rapport with the student in terms of how I was able to quickly forge connections. He cautioned me, however, that my sweater was too low cut, and he was concerned that it could potentially trigger the child's past sexual misconduct. Establishing professional and clear physical boundaries includes determining how close one sits and how one situates one's body in relation to the interviewee. Consult your supervisor when interviewing minors so you will be sure to set up a physical space that is conducive to interviewing appropriately and to discuss how to establish professional boundaries with interviewees.

The tone and cadence of the interviewer's voice make a big impact when questions are posed. Think about modulating your *pitch* (high, medium, low), *affect* (calm, neutral, energetic), and *clarity* (enunciated vs. mumbled words) when pilot-testing your interview protocol in preparation for actual interviews. The auditory quality of the interviewer's voice also affects the recording quality and hence the ability to produce clear transcriptions.

During the interview, be flexible and ready for the unexpected. Sometimes people get excited or emotional or change their minds about being interviewed. For example, Kelly-Corless (2020) was interviewing d/Deaf prisoners and had to find tissues when one person started crying. She also found it challenging to conduct the interview in the constant presence of the prison official, which led to a lack of privacy as well as interruptions.

For Step 10, ask yourself:

- How do I cultivate trust and rapport leading up to and while conducting the interview?
- Am I a member of the community to which the interviewee belongs? If not, do I need to work with another interviewer who is a member of that community to conduct the interview?

Step 11: Record the Interview

Recording is important for verifying what was said during the interview. Listening to the interview multiple times and providing a record of the interview allows you to subject it to memoing, coding, and further analysis. Various methods of audio and video capture are available. Each type of recording device, whether analog or digital, with or without built-in transcription functions, must be approved in the human subjects protocol and used consistently across all the interviews. Data should be password encrypted or stored on an encrypted device. Sometimes a neutral third-party broker can be used to keep a record of names of interviewees with the associated pseudonym; that way, the researcher and research team do not know the original or authentic identity of the interview transcriptions.

In Chapter 5, I discuss how digital interview files can be transcribed by a professional transcriptionist or by the interviewer. Other options include using software with built-in transcription for closed-captioning purposes, such as Zoom (https://zoom.us/) or Otter.ai (https://otter.ai/). These transcriptions will likely need additional cleaning to clarify words that the software misinterprets, such as names, places, and terms with nuanced meanings.

If you have never transcribed an interview, try it: You will get a precious second chance to hear the interviewee contemplate your questions, reflect on them, and respond. You will be able to note valuable pauses; intonations; and expressions, such as small laughs. You will also be able to reflect on your own interviewing abilities and think about the pacing of the questions, the ordering of each question, and the cadence of the overall interview.

Online interviewing is used to reach people who are not in close geographic proximity to your research location or cannot be interviewed because of specific constraints, such as busy schedules, different time zones, illness, bans on face-to-face research (e.g., due to COVID-19), or other factors. Although several types of online meeting services can be used, such as Google Meet (https://meet.google.com), Skype (https://www.skype.com), and GoToMeeting (https://www.goto.com/meeting), it's important to make sure these are compliant with the Health Insurance

Portability and Accountability Act of 1996 (HIPAA). At the time of this writing, the video conference platform Zoom includes a HIPAA-compliant feature for those doing research at colleges and universities.

For Step 11, ask yourself:

- What recording device best suits the interview situation?
- What transcription options do I have, and how will I ensure accuracy of the transcription?

Step 12: Take Notes and Memos

Oftentimes it is helpful to print out the interview protocol and note questions that were important, ones that need more discussion for a follow-up interview, or perhaps ones you were not able to cover because of time limitations. I like to clip a copy of the protocol to a clipboard; I do not advise using your phone or laptop because it can interfere with building rapport. Jot down little notes on stickies, or use a simple, lined notebook before, during, and after the interview. *Memos* are a qualitative research method of writing down reflections on the interviewing process and topics you are researching. Committing to regular memo (sometimes called *journal*) entries can help clarify how research transforms the researcher (see Malacrida, 2007). Some social scientists use a field notebook to organize thoughts on research projects. These are much like a diary, but they pertain solely to the development of the research, theories, and next steps. Here are some writing exercises to help you develop your memos about the interview process:

- **Memo after your first interview.** As soon after the interview as possible, while your memory is fresh, write up your notes about the interview. Describe your overall impression, and take note of which questions seemed to fall flat and which evoked the most response or generated the most interest (Luttrell, 2010). Some researchers take photographs of places and people to bridge what they hear about in interviews to their analysis (Spradley, 1979).
- **Memo about the interview transcript.** After listening to the interview several times, make a list of points about which you think you need

more clarification, questions you wish you had asked, and issues you would want to pursue. Then transcribe the most interesting parts of the interview. Spend time rereading the transcript, and write a memo about it. Why have you selected these parts? Is there a theme, a trend, or a key distinction that has grabbed your attention (Luttrell, 2010)? Researchers have a tendency to simplify language and lose cultural meaning (Spradley, 1979); therefore, highlight verbatim special phrases or terms.

- **Memo to summarize the interview.** Write a letter to the interviewee that summarizes what you learned from the interview. Do not use any of the interviewee's own words, only your restatements (Luttrell, 2010). This is called a *condensed account* of the interview (Spradley, 1979).
- **Memo about teaming.** Write a memo about your participation in a new team project. Describe what experience you've had with qualitative research, what your expectations are, what your epistemological framework is, what your stake in the research is, and perhaps even what your concerns are (C. A. Barry et al., 1999).

For Step 12, ask yourself:

- What note-taking method best suits the interview setup?
- What kind of memos will be useful?

Now that you've connected your interview questions to your research topic, fleshed out your interview protocol, and conducted an interview, you're off to a strong start! Your first few interviews will get you into a rhythm that sets the stage for completing a larger set of interviews. If you are conducting focus groups, Chapter 3 introduces you to basic steps similar to the ones covered for interviews. Chapter 4 shows you how to combine interview and focus group data and how to integrate these data with a quantitative strand. If you are using interviews only this time around, you can skip forward to Chapter 5, which focuses on ensuring rigor, validity, and reliability in your research study.

3

Focus Groups

Do you remember going to your first college class? Just like going to your first job interview, talking in groups can also be a little (or a lot) nerve-racking. Sometimes professors and teachers feel nervous teaching to groups, too. At first, that's how both focus group participants and moderators might feel. For these reasons, conducting a focus group may be even more daunting than doing an interview. In addition, it's a bit hard to decide whether an interview versus a focus group is better for your research project. So, in this chapter I help you prepare for conducting a focus group and help you decide whether to do an interview or a focus group or both.

Simply defined, *focus groups* are socially constructed speech acts that give researchers valuable insight into perspectives and interpersonal interactions in a group setting. Much like interviews, the focus group moderator poses questions, and individuals comment about their perspectives,

https://doi.org/10.1037/0000299-004
How to Interview and Conduct Focus Groups, by J. Katz-Buonincontro

experiences, thoughts, values, and opinions. The key difference between individual interviews and focus groups is that focus group members can "riff," or build off of each other's ideas; discuss a topic or debate; and disagree with each other.

Focus group moderation skills build on interviewing skills in that they also require the researcher to think on the fly when posing questions and handling unexpected responses. However, the difference is, with more than one research participant in the room (or on a video conference), the number of responses increases. That's why running a focus group requires facilitation skills and knowledge about group process, on top of everything else an interviewer would do in a one-on-one format.

This chapter offers eight steps that will take you through designing, planning, and conducting a focus group. You will also learn tips for managing the tensions that naturally arise between participants' commonalities (*homogeneity*) and differences (*heterogeneity*). Honoring this tension means you are creating conditions for people to construct robust responses. Diminishing that tension, or letting it get out of hand, however, may lead to a lack of helpful data or to participants feeling unable to voice their own thoughts—or even feeling silenced by others in the group.

WHY AND WHEN IS IT HELPFUL TO COLLECT GROUP (VS. INDIVIDUAL) RESPONSES TO QUESTIONS?

The potential benefits of focus groups are many. Asking questions to a group of people in a structured focus group allows you, as the researcher, to get a sense of the voice of people in a group setting. The people in a focus group may all be reflecting on a singular experience, such as seeking medical services at a new clinic, or they may be talking about a collective group experience, such as taking a class together.

Groups can have a powerful and positive effect on their members. As people share their thoughts, they surface new perspectives that might otherwise have been latent or hidden in a one-on-one interview. Above all, it's important that focus group members do not feel coerced into creating a consensus about their views (Krueger & Casey, 2009). In fact, heterogeneity or diversity of thought are the sine qua non of focus groups.

In the 1930s, social scientists developed focus group methods as an alternative to questionnaires because of a concern that researchers ask leading questions that may foster passivity in study participants (Rice, 1931). This means that the validity of people's perceptions came into question: How can a person's true thoughts be captured by a questionnaire when they do not have the chance to construct their own responses? During World War II, military psychologists used focus groups to investigate the efficacy of radio programs to boost army morale (Berg, 2004). From there, the use of focus groups spread to marketing. For example, in the 1950s, marketing researchers used focus groups to test consumer preferences for certain products (Merriam, 2009). K. Merton et al. (1956) developed focus groups to concentrate on grouping people who have knowledge of a certain subject. Through this common body of knowledge, people were able to provide context about their experiences and develop collective input for the researcher. When people have common experiences on which group members can elaborate together, focus groups can draw out how these experiences (or opinions and beliefs) contrast. As a result, the data represent a wider range of views than data gained from a single interview. The essential steps listed next dig deeper into additional benefits of focus groups.

ESSENTIAL STEPS IN CONDUCTING A FOCUS GROUP

Two key principles lay the foundation for an effective, high-quality focus group: (a) homogeneity of a common group characteristic and (b) heterogeneity of thought. A *homogeneous grouping characteristic*, such as "museum-goer," provides a way to select people across various strata, such as age, gender, race, income level, occupation, and education level, for a focus group. *Heterogeneity of thought* means successfully moderating a focus group to allow for freely articulated thoughts and diverse opinions. In the example of museum-goers, combining the two principles would reveal different reasons for going to a museum and various preferences for types of exhibitions discussed by each focus group member. Building heterogeneity into homogeneous groupings leads to authentic, valid focus group data.

Step 1: Clarify the Focus Group's Purpose and Orientation

Clarifying the purpose and orientation of the focus group starts with reflecting on why a focus group might be a better method for your study than an interview. Choosing between an interview or a focus group is a common dilemma in qualitative research. Each has advantages and trade-offs. Interviews are good for in-depth, one-on-one discussions to delve into historical, personal, or sensitive beliefs, perspectives, values, and opinions that are not affected by other people's discussion of their thoughts. As explored in Chapter 2, interviews can focus on story-making (narrative) or customs inherent to cultures (ethnography), for example.

Focus groups, on the other hand, are not an avenue for such immersive inquiry; instead, they allow people to speak about common experiences and interests in a convivial, supportive forum. Experiences and perspectives take a broader view of the basis for behavior, whereas attitudes and opinions are considered to be brief(er) segments of thought (Morgan, 1997). Focus groups afford you the ability to collect data when you have only one chance to speak to a special group gathered together or when you do not have enough time to conduct multiple individual interviews (Berg, 2004). They also allow you to seize the opportunity to capture a unique place-based event (e.g., a tornado) or a critical historical occurrence (e.g., a peaceful protest).

Let's say you are interested in gathering experiences and perspectives as a first stage of research, and then you will delve later into attitudes and opinions. Depending on the nature of the study and the comfort level of the participants, you can ask the study participants if they would prefer an individual interview or if they would rather speak as part of a focus group. Chapter 4 includes more information about research designs that combine interviews and focus groups and how to combine one or both qualitative methods with quantitative methods. As you determine what you want to get out of the focus group—that is, your purpose—it can also help to think about how you will set up your groups and orient them to the topic you'd like them to discuss.

Providing an *extended focus group* is the administration of a detailed questionnaire before the actual focus group (Berg, 2004). This primes the focus group members, so they start thinking about the topics to be discussed. It also serves as a quantitative source of data that can shape the grouping of individuals in each focus group according to their particular responses. Last, the survey data can be compared with the focus group themes in a report or manuscript.

Creating a touchstone is a way for the focus group moderator to explore a common topic or experience in the conversation (Tracy, 2013). For example, the moderator may want to discuss the catalyst for a peaceful protest and ask focus group members what inspired them to take part. In this case, the touchstone would be "inspiration for protesting." An image of inspiration, such as an artistic rendition of a heart or a photograph of people engaged in protests, might be used as the touchstone, to help kick off discussion, for example. Another example of a touchstone used in focus groups is a hospital visit experience for youth who had attempted suicide (Mulvale et al., 2021). The hospital visit experience in the focus group allowed members to share emotional pain and build cross-cutting experiences. Without a touchstone, focus groups can be disjointed. If you cannot imagine creating a touchstone in a focus group, then an individual interview might better serve your research purpose.

Bracketing (Hursserl, 1966/1991), or raising up a special concept, is a technique characteristic of phenomenology. Inspecting a concept among the focus group members allows them to discuss a concept in depth. By inspecting a concept together in a group setting, focus group members can delve deeply into their opinions. For example, the moderator might want to pause the group to zero in on a particular concept raised by group members, such as the concept of "good medical care." The moderator might ask questions to pull apart the idea of good medical care by asking what it feels like to be cared for, valued, and heard when seeking medical services. Bracketing is a way to respond organically to new issues raised by focus group members, similar to being open to unexpected interview responses, as discussed in Chapter 2.

As you work through Step 1, ask yourself:

- Which focus group strategy (extended focus group, touchstone, bracketing) best fits my project?

Step 2: Select a Homogeneous Grouping Characteristic

Once you've clarified the reason for choosing a focus group, select a homogeneous grouping characteristic. This means pondering the key criteria for sampling focus group members. To begin, consider the sample size. Sample size is an important consideration for focus groups because of the implications for moderating them. Focus groups can range from three to seven, to even 10, people (Creswell, 2008; Krueger & Casey, 2009). Also, several focus groups with different participants can be conducted on the same research topic. When groups are larger, and if you're new to facilitating groups, the discussion has the potential to become less detailed, or even a bit contrived (Krueger & Casey, 2009), because it's easier to miss each person's contribution. Focus groups typically last about 90 minutes to 2 hours. Studies often offer payment to each member, in exchange for their time, or arrange for a meal or snacks to be served. Child care or respite care can help potential participants who are full-time caregivers.

Once you have determined the study sample, how do you decide who should be in each focus group, what is called the *grouping characteristic*? Oftentimes we default to people's availability. However, there are special ways to assign people to focus groups.

Researchers conduct focus groups with either naturally occurring groups of individuals or individuals who do not know each other. Examples of people who may already be grouped according to enrollment might be patients in a clinic, clients in a special program, students taking a certain class, members of a professional organization, or peers in a student organization. Semitransient populations are also considered for focus groups, such as prisoners; migrant workers; parents at parent–teacher association meetings; or those attending one-time events, such as conventions (Berg, 2004). Homogeneity of a similar grouping characteristic might be "museum-goer," "conservative Republican," "school district employee," or "product user," but the group itself might range in age, gender, race, socioeconomic status, or organizational role.

Be careful to consider whether there are preexisting conflicts across group members because of previous interactions or power differentials due to rank in an organization or other factors. As a result, you might want to have a homogeneous grouping characteristic such as "experience with diversity initiative" and then form focus groups by subset, such as parent, teacher, student, and community member. As with interviews and other types of data, use a human subjects protocol application to gain permission from your institution's institutional review board (see Chapter 1).

As you work through Step 2, ask yourself:

- What's the best way to cluster focus group members?

Step 3: Designate a Moderator

Researchers often choose to identify and designate a special focus group moderator other than themselves to manage the focus group in order to allow them to passively observe the group interactions and take notes. This allows the researcher to learn about how participants interact as they discuss a specific issue. In this way, the social construction of talk is highlighted. If you are not the moderator, then you can observe *how* people talk, not just what they are talking about. For example, in a workplace bullying study, Tracy (2013) observed, but did not moderate, the focus group and found it revealing that people in focus groups exhibited certain commanding behaviors during the actual group sessions.

Reach out to administrators who work with the populations from which you expect to recruit to act as liaisons and possible moderators of focus groups. This might involve asking administrators who have special skills or certifications, such as speaking a certain language, working with special populations, or living in the community with which you would like to work. In this case, the liaison might have insider status with the group you would like to recruit. When necessary, consider how to use inclusivity in the recruitment process. Insider status might mean having similar attributes, such as language, or other special characteristics, such as gender, ethnicity, or race.

Moderators with insider status can complement the aims of the focus groups. For example, research conducted in other countries can benefit from including researchers and group members from those communities. Pramualratana et al. (1985, cited in Morgan, 1997) worked with Thai families in their rural communities to ask about raising families. The research team included members of the community and held the focus groups in the communities instead of at university locations.

Although insider status may help elicit focus group data, it can also work against the aims of the study. For example, Krueger and Casey (2009) reported how American Indian focus group moderators obtained different information from Caucasian American focus group moderators in a study of cardiovascular health in American Indian communities. The American Indian moderators were familiar with some of the health barriers, so they did not probe the participants to describe what they meant. Conversely, the Caucasian American moderators were unfamiliar with the health barriers, so they asked comparatively more questions to elicit more detailed descriptions and information about the health barriers. As a result, different data were collected from the groups: The first group concealed their health barriers, but the second group revealed theirs.

Moderators might also have a special skill set for facilitating focus groups. For example, Crowe (2003) asked a facilitator with expertise in American Sign Language to conduct a focus group with participants who had hearing impairments. Some of the participants could hear with assistive devices and speak their responses, whereas others preferred to sign.

The moderator supported all group members by allowing each to communicate using their natural language preferences.

For Step 3, ask yourself:

- Who would be a good moderator?
- What characteristics would they bring to moderation?

Step 4: Develop a Focus Group Guide

A *focus group guide* is an extensive protocol, longer than the average interview protocol. The guide includes setting aside time in the focus group for five sections: (a) an introduction, (b) basic guidelines, (c) questions, (d) activities, and (e) conclusion. Unlike interviews, focus group members react to ideas presented by another member of the focus group, thus generating a rich range of heterogeneous responses and occasionally getting off track. That's why a guide is a good resource. Focus group guides have multiple layers of questions that are segmented with breaks. A typical focus group guide includes these five sections, each of which is described next.

Introduction

The introduction to the project foregrounds the questions. Focus group participant roles are described. Participants can introduce themselves to the group. The moderator can ask them to identify a favorite hobby or flavor of ice cream, for example, depending on the group. This helps relax the group and build rapport between the moderator and the group. Consent forms can be distributed and explained.

Guidelines

As when teaching a class, it is important to set the ground rules for participant behavior and expectations, to create a climate of mutual respect. Discuss the norms as outlined in the moderation principles. You can email these norms in advance, print them out, or post them on a whiteboard. This is especially important when discussing potentially sensitive topics, such as relationships, substance use, patient care, personal identity, or homelessness, for example. You may want to develop warm-up questions and more generalized questions that would precede questions on sensitive topics. An example focus group protocol on racial identity and socioeconomic status is presented in Table 3.1.

Questions

The questions prompt discussion across the group. Generally speaking, they differ from intensive interview questions. Focus group questions typically are relatively short, as opposed to lengthy or long winded, to spur conversation. To develop the questions, you can consult the question stem and question extension examples given in Chapter 2. There is a general pattern to focus group questions that includes an opening, introduction, transition, key questions, and ending questions (see Table 3.2; Krueger & Casey, 2009). As with interview questions, pilot-test the questions for various ways to improve the tone, content, flow, and sequence (see Chapter 2 to revisit the guidelines about question stems and prompts).

Table 3.1

Example Focus Group Questions on Racial and Socioeconomic Status

Type of question	Questions
Opening	1. General background questions: age, place of birth
Introductory	2. Where were you raised? 3. What was your neighborhood like? 4. Was it integrated?
Transition	5. How would you define your class background? 6. What was the class background of the family in which you were raised? 7. How would you define your class background? 8. How do you define yourself ethnically? 9. What meaning do you, or does your family, attach to your ethnicity? 10. Are these things ethnically important: holidays, food, dating, neighborhood dynamics?
Key	11. What does it mean to be White in the United States today?
Ending	12. Are you conscious of being White?

Note. Data from Gallagher (1999).

Table 3.2

Focus Group Behavioral Cues and Moderator Comments

Behavioral cue	Moderator comment
Nodding, shaking head, smiling	I notice you were [*nodding/shaking your head/smiling*]; would you care to share your thoughts?
Silence	We've learned a great deal about [*insert subject*], but we have not heard from everyone. [*Name*], can you comment on [insert subject]?
Long or intense conversation	We've talked a lot; let's take a short break. Let's return at 2:15 p.m.
Arguing	Everyone gets a chance to voice their opinion. Let's respect each other and refrain from interruption. Please take turns when speaking. Thank you.
Fatigue	We have a lull in our conversation. Let's take this opportunity to switch the subject. (or) Let's play a short game.
Confusing discussion	I'm not sure what each person is saying. Perhaps I don't get everything you are saying. Could you repeat your point? [*Be careful to use a gentle—not a brusque—tone*]
Side talking	Let's pause our side discussion and get back to the group. [*Offer sticky pads to jot down notes*]
Getting on a tangent	We are getting a little off track; let's circle back to the question again. Let's return to that point a bit later, when we get to that topic.
Distress	I sense a little stress/need for a break; let's take a break and then resume. [*Offer tissue or bottle of water*]

One exception to the multiple-question protocol is David Morgan's *single-question strategy.* In one study, Morgan (1997) asked, "What kinds of things have made being widowed either easier or harder for you?" This question was sufficiently broad and open-ended to spur enough conversation for 2 hours in each of six focus groups. When a researcher is seasoned and has substantial background knowledge, including familiarity with recent research on the topic, this approach can work well. If you are starting out in qualitative research and new to the method of focus groups, you will want to have a core question, preceded by warm-up questions and followed by concluding questions, written out before you begin.

If you have a moderator, be sure to review the questions with them before the first focus group is held. Ensure that the questions are relatively short, and do not use complicated words or jargon. The questions should be easy to read. Also, avoid *double-tailed questions* (i.e., when two questions are combined into one). Focus groups also give moderators a unique opportunity to poll people about their opinions (e.g., using the question stem "On a scale of 1 to 5, how would you rate [the quality of your recent therapy] . . .?"; Tracy, 2013). You can introduce a topic by presenting a short set of predetermined responses and then ask focus group members to raise their hand to respond.

Also consider the tone of focus group questions. Begin groups with a welcoming tone, and word questions in a positive manner that does not assume the group members have only negative experiences. Groups who share a marginalized identity require respect, special care, and attention on the part of the researcher. For example, a focus group moderator working with a group of teen parents would want to pay close attention to the relationships the parents have fostered over time in building a positive identity despite the negative barriers they have faced in their lives, in schools, and in larger society.

Art and Photovoice Activities

Researchers can layer creative learning activities into a focus group protocol, either before or during the actual focus group. For example, architects conducting community focus groups for designing a new public library might plan out a *photovoice activity*, asking participants to take photos of places where youth like to spend time in the community. Participants can add captions or descriptions to the photos that describe the youth activities and then bring the photos to the focus group to share and discuss. Similarly, the researcher might ask the participants to log the list of places in the community they have visited over the duration of 1 week or keep a journal about what and where they like to read.

For materials, you might want to give each focus group member a pen, some paper, a stack of sticky notes, and/or a small personal whiteboard, so they can jot down thoughts before responding to a question in the group. Not all focus groups have special activities, but they help break up longer focus groups and give people an opportunity to participate in an activity together.

Example activities include photographs (CohenMiller, 2018), role playing, improvisation, drawing with captions (Lopez et al., 2018), and playing a short game. Focus group members can draw maps to generate metaphors (Foster et al., 2018). To build leadership in youth who feel unempowered in a focus group, they can draw pictures of themselves (Mulvale et al., 2021).

Another activity option is to use political cartoons or photographs from a newspaper and ask participants what comes to mind when they look at the picture. These activities change the tempo of the focus group, and they can uplift the mood and help facilitate thinking in a different way through interpretation or artistic expression. Art performances can also occur after a focus group; for example, Hodgins (2017) worked with playwrights and actors to develop a play derived from a focus group of brain injury survivors.

Conclusion

Wrapping up a focus group means providing a summary of key points to the group members. This allows them to feel heard, reflect on their thoughts, and validate the data you are collecting. The moderator can use a whiteboard to write out key themes and provide a copy of notes digitally to each focus group member.

For Step 4, ask yourself:

- Have I included all necessary sections in my focus group guide?
- What, if any, activities will help the group members engage in the discussion?

Step 5: Develop a Group Agreement for Maintaining Confidentiality

Focus groups often use group agreements for maintaining confidentiality within focus group members in addition to signing consent forms. This is key for protecting the disclosure of private information discussed among members. Exhibit 3.1 shows an example of a simple agreement that can be tailored to your research project.

Exhibit 3.1

Group Agreement

This form is intended to further ensure confidentiality of data obtained during the study conducted by [insert name of investigator here]. All focus group members in addition to the focus group moderator will be asked to read the following statement and sign their names indicating that they agree to comply:

I hereby affirm that I will not communicate or in any manner disclose publicly information discussed during the course of this focus group. I agree not to talk about material relating to this study or focus group outside of my fellow focus group members and the researcher and moderator.

Name: _____

Signature: _____

Principal Investigator/Researcher: _____

Note. Data from Berg (2004).

For Step 5, ask yourself:

- Why is confidentiality important for the group?

Step 6: Use Effective Facilitation Principles

Have you ever run a meeting or taught a class? It can be exhilarating, but it does take careful planning, preparation, and energy. Instead of devoting one's attention to one person in an interview, focus group researchers spread their attention to each person in the focus group and their interactions.

Focus groups are generally much smaller than college classes, with about five to 10 participants (Krueger & Casey, 2009). In some cases, they can be larger. For your own research project, aim for a manageable size, keeping inclusivity in mind. *Inclusivity* involves recruiting as many persons as possible without preferential treatment, as well as providing time for each person to answer the questions without being talked over or treated negatively. The key principles for effective facilitation of focus groups are psychological safety, respect, equal airtime, and heterogeneity of thought.

Psychological Safety

Openly discuss group agreements or expectations of behavior at the outset of the focus group to help members feel safe psychologically. With a group, you are signaling two things: First, you care about their well-being during the focus group. Second, you want each member to uphold principles of fairness when speaking to each other during the focus group.

Respect

Mutual respect during discussions is essential. Focus group participants need to use respectful language that does not show undue bias or discrimination. Participants who disrespect other participants should be asked to leave the room and discontinue participation.

Equal Airtime

Just like traditional classroom discussions, it is important to allow each focus group member to talk. Letting someone hog the mic is not fair to other members. Provide this guideline to everyone so that all perspectives are honored and given fair representation through enough time to speak. You may need to interrupt respectfully and come back to frequent talkers later. Remind them that they are free to jot down notes as they listen. Equal airtime is critical for fostering heterogeneity of responses across focus group members. In Chapter 4, I discuss heterogeneity in more depth, as a principle of validity for focus groups when reporting results.

Heterogeneity of Thought

As discussed at the beginning of this chapter, heterogeneity of thought among participants is a key principle for effective focus groups. Moderators should focus on creating a dynamic environment to foster heterogeneous contributions, one in which people have the opportunity to make comments and even to brainstorm collectively. You can let focus group members know that it is okay to be active thinkers and to communicate freely with each other, as long as the principles of psychological safety, respect, and equal airtime are followed. Carefully consider the age and background of the focus group members. It is important to let young people know that you are not looking for them to affirm one main way, or a popular way, of thinking. Although your job isn't to stoke disagreement, neither is it to encourage *groupthink*, or one centralized way of considering a topic.

For Step 6, ask yourself:

- What conditions will make the focus group successful?

Step 7: Set Up the Focus Group Room

Planning and preparation with respect to proper equipment and space for a focus group are more elaborate than arranging individual interviews. Some universities have dedicated focus group rooms with repositionable large tables, chairs, whiteboards, and built-in mics. It's a great idea to do a dry run of a focus group before it happens, with a friend, research class, or your academic supervisor.

Room Reservations

First, check in with the sign-up system and administrator to reserve the room. Sign up to use the focus group room ahead of time, so you can set up any needed supplies or audiovisual equipment. Locate the restrooms in the building for your guests. For participants who have a driver or caregiver not participating in the actual focus group, provide a couch, lobby area, or other comfy spot where they can wait while the group is in session. As mentioned earlier, if participants will need child care, make all necessary arrangements for that at a nearby location. Direct focus group participants to the room with signage on buildings, walls, elevators, and security guard desks. Work with security guards by providing them a list of approved focus group participants.

Virtual Focus Groups

Virtual focus groups are ideal for convening people who live far apart or who cannot participate together because of health or safety reasons (e.g., COVID-19). Zoom (https://zoom.us/), Google Meet (https://meet.google.com), Skype (https://zoom.us/), Microsoft Teams (https://www.microsoft.com/en-us/microsoft-teams/video-conferencing), GoToMeeting (https://www.goto.com/meeting), and other software platforms can be used to hold virtual focus groups. Within each platform, special tools can be used to record audio. Moderating large groups online can be harder than doing so in person. For example, only a small number of persons will show on one main screen in a Zoom session; as a result, those who join late are pushed to a second or third screen, leading to exclusion issues. On the whole, it is thus advisable to keep smaller groups of three or four for virtual focus groups.

Closed captioning can produce automatically generated transcriptions. Some things to consider are whether free or licensed versions of the software are best to use. For instance, free versions are limited to shorter durations and fewer tools. Smaller breakout "rooms" in each platform are not necessarily ideal for focus groups because you cannot record those discussions. The mute function is important for designating who can speak. Using video as opposed to only the audio function is another critical option: Some people may not be able to use video or feel comfortable doing so. As a result, you should develop virtual participation guidelines to address expectations, including consent to be videotaped. You can also play gentle background music when people first enter the video conference, as they situate themselves. Be sure to go over the software's features and test the tools with participants, to get them comfortable with the online platform, before asking questions. Be sure to press "Record" prior to starting the focus group.

Seating

In face-to-face focus groups, arrange the seating in a comfortable fashion depending on the number of group members, and decide ahead of time whether you want to sit in a circle to promote dialogue. You may want space for role playing, for example, or for small groups to speak with each other.

Incentives and Payment

If you are including payment, plan for distribution at the end of the session. Marketing research companies have a history of providing payment, especially for "elite" or high-wage earners. However, your university might have money allocated for paying participants, especially if the study is not funded by a grant. Therefore, it might be appropriate to consider course credit when possible and appropriate, as approved by the institutional review board. Also, alternative gifts for compensating focus group members related to the study topic, such as a meaningful memento or swag, accompanied with a handwritten note, might be appropriate. Books or gift cards might be appealing if the budget allows.

Refreshment

With face-to-face focus groups, coordinate refreshment, so it is prepared for the arrival of the group members. If you do not have snacks, consider providing bottled water for longer groups.

Name Tags

As focus group members enter the room in face-to-face focus groups, provide colorful pens and name tags to attach to their clothing. This is a fun way for people to mingle. Conversely, you can print out name tags if it is necessary to save time.

For Step 7, ask yourself:

- What logistics and items do I need to prepare in advance for the focus group?

Step 8: Conduct the Focus Group

With focus groups, it's all hands on deck for the research team. In addition to the designated focus group moderator, researchers need help setting up the room, welcoming guests, and running the technology to ensure quality recording. In rooms designed for focus groups, there may be microphones and video cameras located in the ceilings and walls, or you may need to arrange for these to be brought in. Learn how to operate them before the actual focus group. Depending on the options available, decide whether you will use audio or video or both. If you decide to use audio only, remember to ask focus group participants to state their name before talking, to identify who is speaking and to help ensure clarity in the transcription and coding process; this will ensure validity of the data.

Record Confidential Data

If data are to be confidential, focus group members can choose a number or pseudonym to represent them. They can write their preferred name on a name tag.

Start the Recording

Don't forget to start the recording before you begin welcoming everyone as they arrive. This is important, especially if you have latecomers. In addition, make sure your recording devices are plugged into a socket, and consider bringing the correct type of batteries as a backup source of power, in addition to a recording device such as a video camera, smartphone, or computer.

Set a Welcoming Tone

Remember that you as the moderator want to make everyone feel comfortable at the start of the focus group. Provide a little soft jazz or other type of music in the background as people arrive.

Note Your Affect

If people do not know each other, start off the focus group gently. Think about your own affect and whether you exude relaxation or tension. Your mood may affect the focus group members and possibly their answers.

Encourage Quiet People to Participate

It's hard to anticipate who will be talkative and who will be reticent. If you notice someone is quiet, they may be formulating their answers, or they may feel shy.

Refrain From Formulations

It can be tempting to reformulate focus group participant comments in such a way that may bias the conversation (Tracy, 2013). Try to stay neutral and let people finish speaking without interruptions. If you accidentally cut someone off, you can adjust the discussion accordingly and apologize if need be.

Don't Ignore Distress

If a focus group member displays worry or stress or tears up, don't ignore it. Offer to help, provide tissues, and let the person know they can take a breather, or a break, and then resume talking when comfortable.

Make Note of the Seating

While the moderator is facilitating the group, the researcher or a research assistant or team member can make a rough diagram noting who sits where. This helps trigger memory about the nature of the conversation and of who spoke when.

For Step 8, ask yourself:

- How can I set up a professional tone and climate for the focus group that is also supportive and welcoming?

Empathy for other points of view, noticing key behavioral cues, and solving problems on the fly to accommodate unusual or unexpected comments are three core skills essential to focus group moderation. Crafting group agreements and developing and pilot-testing a protocol will help offset or mitigate the challenges to focus group moderation. Art or photovoice activities prime focus group members to think deeply about core issues and engage them in the reflection process. Bracketing and using a touchstone help further focus the discussion around potentially sensitive and personal issues. Planning the physical setup requirements, whether for a face-to-face group or one conducted via a software platform, is key. In the end, focus group facilitation—much like teaching or presenting—can be quite fun.

4

Combining Interviews and Focus Groups and Mixing Methods

When might it be important to combine interviews and focus groups? Focus groups and interviews can be conducted, analyzed, and reported as stand-alone data in a study or combined together in one study. In this chapter, I give you tips and strategies for deciding when and how to combine them.

There are many ways to combine interviews and focus groups that play to the strengths of each method. For example, one could use a qualitative case study design starting with focus groups of clients who have completed different therapies. Interviews could then be conducted with the clients to examine their specific experiences with therapy by engaging them in multiple individual interviews. Table 4.1 provides a summary of 11 possible ways to combine data types in a study and how to sequence the data. It also lists the benefits of each.

https://doi.org/10.1037/0000299-005
How to Interview and Conduct Focus Groups, by J. Katz-Buonincontro

Table 4.1

Eleven Ways to Combine Data

Research purpose	Data sequence		Potential benefits of data combination
	First	Second	
1. Discuss sensitive topics	Focus groups or interviews		■ Allow for participants to specify preference to incentivize participation ■ Foster community inclusion ■ Schedule flexibility ■ Location preference
2. Deepen discussions	Focus group	Interviews	■ Develop trust and rapport ■ Enhance authenticity of data
3. Group compatible people	Interview	Focus group	■ Increase participants' comfort level
4. Develop new survey items	Focus group or interview	Survey	■ Establish cultural validity ■ Strengthen construct validity ■ Avoid specification error
5. Pilot-test survey	Survey	Focus group or interview	■ Increase reliability
6. Explain survey results	Survey	Focus group or interview	■ Refine the qualitative research question ■ Determine purposive sample ■ Craft the interview/focus group protocol ■ Enrich the explanation of results
7. Test a tool	Focus group	Survey	■ Examine the usability of a new tool, curriculum, or software ■ Provide iterative feedback at multiple stages ■ Elicit expert opinions of stakeholders about tool
8. Identify a new observation site	Focus group	Observation	■ Increase site access ■ Develop liaison relationships to the sites
9. Member-check results	Observation	Focus group	■ Increase validity ■ Confirmatory

	Table 4.1		
	Eleven Ways to Combine Data (*Continued*)		
Research purpose	Data sequence		Potential benefits of data combination
	First	Second	
10. Develop interventions	Focus group	Intervention	■ Develop buy-in ■ Recruit and enroll community members
11. Provide feedback across treatment and control groups	Random control trial intervention (two armed)	Focus group	■ Compare experiences ■ Enhance successful impact ■ Refine future interventions ■ Understand barriers to delivering interventions

Social scientists sometimes examine a topic from both a qualitative and a quantitative perspective and then integrate the results to form a third, mixed-methods perspective. Mixed-methods projects might use focus groups, interviews, or qualitative observations in conjunction with census data, survey data, quantitative observations, or even randomized controlled experiments. There's a healthy precedent for mixing methods, although it can be a little daunting, especially if you are new to research.

> In this chapter, you will learn how interviews and focus groups can be used together in one study. You will also read a few examples illustrating how to use them with other types of data in mixed-methods studies. As you read, think about your next research project. Would any of the data collection options described here be a good fit? Why or why not?

COMBINING FOCUS GROUPS AND INTERVIEWS

The benefits of combining focus groups and interviews are many. As mentioned in Chapter 3, sometimes researchers offer the choice to participate in a focus group or an interview. Offering the option fosters inclusion within the community being studied, in particular, when isolation and lack of resources may be barriers to research participation, because it allows flexibility in regard to meeting locations and time schedules. Another benefit of giving participants a choice is that it promotes a sense of comfort when the topic at hand is sensitive. For example, Levesque et al. (2020) allowed participants to select either focus groups or interviews in a study of breast cancer among Chinese Australian women. In their study, participants could select their preferred language (Cantonese or Mandarin). A qualified translator aided the researchers with translation. Focus groups were conducted in a research institute or in the office of a cancer support organization, whereas the interviews took place in the participant's home. This flexibility allowed participants to select the format with which they most felt comfortable to speak about topics such as breast cancer treatment and information resources. Similarly, Gillum (2008) conducted both focus groups and interviews with African American women who had survived domestic abuse. The combination of the two methods allowed Gillum to gather data about a range of intimate experiences, such as perceptions of unfair treatment compared with White women in domestic violence shelters.

Several other methods of combining interview and focus group data are described in the sections that follow, with an emphasis on the benefits of each.

Deepening Focus Group Discussions

Have you ever used a funnel to pour liquid from a large jug into a small bottle? *Funneling* is a metaphor for transitioning from a large quantity to several smaller quantities. In this way, a researcher could use focus groups for touching on broader issues and then select informants to funnel the information into smaller, detailed topics best suited for discussion in an individual interview. As such, focus groups can help researchers expand the range of thoughts examined by allowing them to scrutinize the topic in more depth with individual group members.

In the funneling process, the focus group allows the researcher to get a more general sense of a set of experiences and familiarize themselves with a group of people. Once the focus group is completed, the researcher can follow up and meet with each focus group member to discuss their perspectives in more detail. In this combination, the sequencing of the focus group and then the interviews allows for expansion of the research topic. For example, Markey et al. (2019) used purposive sampling to conduct focus groups with nursing students and discovered that students did not know how to implement culturally responsive care. As a result, they theoretically sampled nurse practitioners in four hospitals to interview. In other words, they sampled groups of nurse practitioners according to their comfort level in implementing culturally responsive care.

Grouping Compatible People on the Basis of Interviews

By reversing the order of data collection just described, researchers can choose to conduct interviews with a relatively wide range of people and then group them into focus groups on the basis of their compatibility (Morgan, 1997). This way, the researcher can use the interviews to explore a topic and then examine the same topic from a group perspective.

For example, one might interview each student in a class about how they characterize their own personal learning style and then group students who have a common characteristic that emerged during the interviews. For instance, learners who indicate in the interviews that they struggle with online learning could be invited to take part in a focus group in which they discuss their struggles with other group members and compare their experiences. This could be a source of new data because the students would potentially further open up and discuss the nature and severity of their online learning struggles.

MIXING DATA: COMBINING FOCUS GROUPS AND INTERVIEWS WITH QUANTITATIVE DATA

Survey data are probably the type of quantitative data most frequently combined with data gained through focus groups and interviews. Research-based intervention studies and program evaluations are two types of studies in which mixed methods are frequently applied.

Developing and Pilot-Testing Surveys

Although many survey studies do not necessarily use formal mixed methods with a purposeful qualitative component, survey researchers always have the option of developing and testing items with focus groups, especially if the topic has not been researched much. When developing a new survey, researchers can explore the range of items to ensure they have covered sufficiently the actual concepts to be measured. Focus group discussions and interviews can elicit new descriptions that the researcher hadn't thought of because of their lack of experience in a specific area. These important dimensions of an experience can lead to the development of a set of new items for a scale on a survey instrument, for example.

Establishing cultural validity is important when one is aiming to ensure culturally sensitive assessment and measurement of diverse cultural groups of people. To be specific, the cognitive meaning and linguistic interpretation of words depend in part on the respondents' cultural backgrounds and contexts. Because of this, survey items do not necessarily have direct translation equivalence across languages. To help ensure cultural validity, researchers translate survey items from a primary language into a secondary language, that is, the one in which the survey will be administered. They then back-translate the survey items into the primary language to ensure careful and accurate translation.

In addition to the process of back-translation, cognitive interviews and focus groups are an appropriate option for culturally relevant research. For example, Agans et al. (2006) used cognitive interviews and focus groups with Mexican women to develop a questionnaire about menstruation in a culturally sensitive manner. First, the focus groups allowed the researchers to discover that the Spanish translation of the term "focus group" itself, *el grupo de foco*, did not make sense to the Mexican women. On the basis of the feedback they received, Agans et al. built in time to explain this method of speaking in groups and made sure to provide a safe and secure environment in which the women could use an alias, or pseudonym. In addition, the focus groups allowed the researchers to choose the best verbs on the basis of the expressions used by the focus group participants, which were informed not only by the Spanish verbs but also by the Mexican cultural context. Last, the focus group allowed the participants to speak about and discuss culturally taboo issues, including menstruation, abuse, and possible medical misdiagnoses due to racism.

The development of domains on a survey relates to how the survey data are analyzed (Morgan, 1997). For example, if a researcher develops a narrow set of scales that misses an important aspect—say, "physical pain when breastfeeding" on an instrument seeking to measure "persistence at breastfeeding"—then a possible consequence is *specification error*. Specification error can result from the omission of a certain independent variable (or inclusion of the wrong independent variable) in a regression model. Multiple regression aims to predict an outcome variable (dependent variable) as explained by independent variables. As a result of this omission, the estimators will be biased in terms of direction and in terms of magnitude (W. D. Barry & Feldman, 1985).

These issues highlight the importance of (a) ensuring proper inclusion of dimensions of the domain under investigation and (b) carefully linking qualitative focus group or interview data to the wording and phrasing of items in a survey.

In addition to using interviews and focus groups to create survey items, the survey pilot-testing process generally includes asking respondents to not only take the survey but also discuss their interpretations of the questions. Typically, only a subset of respondents, not all of them, is asked to discuss their interpretations of the survey questions. Small-group interviews or focus groups allow researchers to methodically examine each question and get direct feedback on how people interpreted the nature of each question. As a result, the researcher can get a more accurate sense of how to best phrase items in the future so as to minimize unreliability (Morgan, 1997). It is important for items to be worded in a relatively simple way that can be comprehended by a wide range of respondents so that ideally, they will respond to the survey items in a more consistent way (e.g., all who agree with a statement will pick "Agree" because they are not confused by the statement), thus likely yielding reliable results.

Explaining Survey Results

After developing and pilot-testing a survey, researchers might want to explain the results with more data: Interviews and focus groups can be used to follow up a survey to help explain the results. In mixed-methods research this is called an *explanatory sequential design* (Creswell & Plano Clark, 2018). It appeals to researchers who prefer to use quantitative research as well as those trying mixed-methods studies for the first time. After collecting and analyzing survey data, the researcher can then refine the qualitative research question and decide to either sample the same group of people or select a smaller purposive group of respondents to conduct focus groups or to interview. The survey results can be used to craft the initial interview or focus group protocol (in which case the approved human subjects protocol can be amended). In addition, the survey results can inform the types of codes used when the transcriptions are examined. In the results stage, focus group or interview data help explain the survey results with *thick*, or detailed, descriptions of certain themes and in vivo, for example, quotes. (In Chapter 5, I discuss strategies to enhance validity using thick description and in vivo quotes.) Focus groups can be used to clarify how the passing of time might change lived experiences; for example, focus groups can also be staged several years after a significant life event, such as a medical procedure, to examine long-term qualitative impacts, especially when only quantitative survey data had been used to study the initial impacts (cf. Malmström et al., 2013).

Identifying Observation Sites

Might people's behaviors and interactions be important for your research? If so, observation can be a powerful complement to focus groups or interviews. Empirical observation can range from direct observation (quantitative to qualitative) to participant observation (qualitative). Observations take place at the participants' location or site, such as a classroom, clinic, public park, or museum. Common barriers to accessing sites such as schools or other institutions include identifying the right time and place to observe an activity relevant to the research topic and getting permission to observe minors as well as professionals who might be overworked, stressed, or just plain busy. Administrators, who may be wary at first, tend to support the idea of observation because it gives an authentic view of how people naturally interact and can showcase potential benefits of and drawbacks to a new program or instructional tool.

Focus groups can be used to explore potential observation sites. Because it takes a while to gain access and establish rapport with sites when conducting research, it can be helpful to conduct focus groups before reaching out to sites and establishing partnerships with them. If this approach is used, one can add as an amendment to an already-approved human subjects protocol onsite letters confirming permission to conduct research. This tactic would generate sampling criteria for the observation site that are based on the focus group members' recommendation.

Member-Checking Observation Results

Member-checking is used in qualitative research as a form of validity to examine the accuracy of interpretation of a focus group's results or participant interview responses, which I explore more deeply in Chapter 5. In addition to this common form of validity, focus groups can be used for confirmatory purposes. An example of this is member-checking observation results in a focus group forum. In this situation, the researcher conducts observations at the research site, analyzes the data qualitatively or quantitatively, and then presents the results to the focus group members. The aim of using the focus group format is to engage in a lengthy discussion of the results as well as confirm (or disconfirm) various results. The focus group data discussing the observation results would then be included in the actual research report.

Program Evaluations, Design Research, and Research-Based Interventions

Program evaluations, design research, and research-based intervention studies use focus groups before or after program services are completed or implemented. Programs implemented in communities sometimes include community members to shape the program, recruit participants, and develop protocols. To that end, focus groups are a great way to include community members during each of these stages. For example, Murdaugh et al. (2000) used focus groups to design an intervention to help HIV-positive women facing issues such as perinatal transmission. The focus group not only provided data about perceptions of pregnancy related to their HIV-positive status but also directly asked women to describe what would be valuable for the purposes of designing a video on the topic specifically as it pertains to cultural relevance.

Designing new use-inspired tools is another way to use focus groups. A *use-inspired tool* is a research-based instrument, device, medicine, or treatment meant to help address a problem in society and have a positive impact on the community, as opposed to just collecting and analyzing data in a journal article, for example, which mostly affects only academia. For example, Levy et al. (2019) invited key stakeholders (therapists) to provide feedback on the potential usability of an electronic grocery store for veterans with mild traumatic brain injury and posttraumatic stress disorder. Focus groups are particularly well suited to design-based research where an iterative process with multiple stages of feedback is needed. In this study, a quantitative scale was also administered to expert stakeholders in the focus groups to measure the usability features of the software.

Research-based interventions also require authentic feedback as to their efficacy and ways to improve community impact. In this case, focus groups held after the implementation of a specific intervention or program can allow researchers to ask about the perceived benefits and drawbacks to the programs or services offered. Focus group data can help ground statistical data for policymakers who are attempting to understand the impact of a program (Morgan, 1997). Donnelly et al. (2013) conducted focus groups of four to five female cancer patients enrolled in a random- ized control trial that included physical therapy. In this study, the focus group moderator was female but did not interact with the patients in the actual trial. The purpose of the focus group was to elicit perceived benefits and challenges of the physical therapy. As a result, two sets of experiences could be compared: those of (a) the treatment/intervention focus group (physical therapy) and (b) the nonintervention group (no physical therapy). Last, the focus group members provided feedback for designing aspects of the intervention for the future (type and duration of treatments, social interaction, and psychological benefits). Other studies have used focus groups to unpack the barriers to delivering interventions (e.g., Martin et al., 2017).

HOW TO DECIDE WHAT TYPES OF DATA TO COLLECT AND IN WHAT SEQUENCE

Let's think through how to combine data and reasons you might choose to do so. First, consider your *design clarity*. Reflect on whether you have a clear reason for using each type of data. Review the basic steps for conducting an interview or a focus group, and think about which one best fits your research question and topic. Also, consider the qualitative design focus and its epistemological framework (ethnography, narrative inquiry, grounded theory, phenomenology, case study, or basic research design; see Chapter 1). Within these designs, recall the specific, unique orientation of the researcher who best suits the larger qualitative design as well as your own research philosophy and communication strengths. In regard to interview methods, there are multiple specialized forms of interviews (individual, dyadic, group) that incorporate various protocols (structured, semistructured, unstructured, didactic), as discussed in Chapter 2. If participants already know each other or have a similar set of experiences, focus groups might be better than interviews. There are many formats for focus groups that can help deepen engagement with the group (e.g., bracketing, creating a touchstone) to facilitate dialogue, including a special group activity (e.g., art).

Next, consider *methodological compatibility*. Look for natural and congruent ways to combine data. Don't force data together if they don't fit. Here are a few guidelines for combining data, which I've summarized in Table 4.1:

- For discussing sensitive topics in which flexibility is the most important participation factor, consider allowing for either focus groups or interviews.

- Focus groups conducted before interviews allow for larger, more general discussion followed by detailed in-depth experiences that might stem from an initial foray into the topic during the focus group. Alternatively, if you conduct interviews first, you can then group people together in a focus group to help increase their comfort level and build camaraderie and hence foster more discussion.

- When developing a new survey for which cultural validity is important, prioritizing qualitative data collection first can strengthen construct validity and avoid specification error. Pilot-testing a survey and following up with a focus group can help increase the reliability, or consistency with which how people answer survey questions.

- Focus groups conducted after the survey can extend, enrich, and elaborate on the results.

- Trying out a new device, software, or treatment in a focus group can provide feedback on a survey.

- On the basis of what the group members say, focus groups can help a researcher explore options for observation sites. Researchers can double-check the accuracy of what they observed with focus group members (this is not a common strategy).

- Focus groups with community members can help develop a new intervention, which is then tested with a new sample that is different than the focus group. After an intervention, focus groups can discuss the intervention and provide valuable feedback to the research team.

With the rapid innovation in ways to combine methods, this is an incredibly exciting time to be a researcher! Sometimes it's like being a kid in a candy store. At first, it seems liberating, even tempting, to try many methods at once. But, just as when you eat too much candy, the choices have consequences. So, as you think through your many options, think also about the time, energy, and other resources available to you. How can you investigate your research questions most efficiently while also ensuring high levels of rigor, validity, and reliability? In Chapter 5, we explore the issues of validity and reliability introduced in this chapter at a more detailed level.

5

Addressing Rigor, Validity, and Reliability

How do we know and communicate whether we're doing research well and in the right way? As researchers, we might work independently, with an advisor or colleague, or as part of a multisite team, so it's important that we have processes and controls for reflecting on the level and dimensions of quality in our work. We also work within a wider, networked community of researchers in organizations, foundations, and review boards who scrutinize our work through peer review, grant reviews, and other processes (e.g., evaluations and human subjects protocol approvals).

Social scientists have developed common understandings about signifiers of rigor and quality, authenticity or validity (truth), and reliability (consistency) to demonstrate sound, credible science. Researchers continue to debate these standards and even whether to describe research as "science." Out of that debate have emerged strong norms that all researchers should consider and to which they should adhere.

https://doi.org/10.1037/0000299-006
How to Interview and Conduct Focus Groups, by J. Katz-Buonincontro

In this chapter, you will learn ways to ensure both validity and reliability during every stage of your project, especially when conducting interviews and focus groups. You will also learn to be aware of the main barriers to validity and how to overcome them.

Qualitative research focuses more on validity than reliability to establish credibility and rigor (Creswell, 2007), so I've chosen to begin this chapter with a presentation of steps to enhance validity and then proceed with steps to address reliability.

STEPS TO ENHANCE RIGOR AND VALIDITY

The concepts of quality and validity are considered at every stage of a research project, not just at the end (Glaser & Strauss, 1967). If something is *authentic* or *valid*, then it is truthful and accurate. Establishing *validity* is the deliberate process of fostering ideas, thoughts, opinions, and perspectives that are true or representative of each participant as conveyed in an interview or a focus group (data collection), representing the results in their totality (data analysis), and making sound inferences on the basis of the results (discussion and implications).

Step 1: Describe the Researcher's Identity and Positionality

As discussed in Chapter 1, building a strong foundation in one's researcher identity and positionality at the outset of the study helps foster validity throughout the processes of design, data collection, analysis, and writing. In addition, describing researcher identity to your research team members and your study participants builds relational trust. In the process of building relational trust, researchers initiate a discussion for disclosing multidimensional and intersectional aspects of their identity and positionality. This exchange in turn signifies respect for the interviewees in terms of acknowledging their position and any privilege accorded to their status and the interviewer's status. This is particularly relevant in identity-based studies, in which one might interview or conduct a focus group on topics of intersectionality, race, gender, or ability, for example.

It is important to acknowledge power imbalances that might arise between the interviewer and the interviewee based on status (academia vs. community membership), rank, gender, race, and ability, for example. The researcher's sincerity and vulnerability will help set the conditions for a high-quality research project (Tracy, 2013), a tradition invoked among other researchers who advocate for the quality of candidness (Wolcott, 1999). For example, in the positionality statement given in Chapter 1 (Exhibit 1.1), the authors pointed toward their position of privilege in terms of belonging to academia and how that accords them social status that may be seen as higher than that of the people they are interviewing, who in this example were immigrants. They also referred to their race and discussed potential differences in their understanding of society and specific issues depending on each person's race. These concepts can be extended to gender and other aspects of identity, depending on the research issue and interview situation. To initiate a discussion about researcher identity, you can ask yourself and your research team some questions:

- How do we each define our individual identities?
- In what ways do academia and the research community reinforce and address power imbalances and/or systemic racism in society?
- Is it necessary for our research team to address these issues with our research participants, and what are some good starting places for initiating these conversations before data collection?

Step 2: Promote Authentic Voice

Authentic voice refers to empowering interviewees and focus group members to assert their voice, especially if they have had experiences in which they felt marginalized because of a feature of their identity. This concept has roots in *egalitarianism*—the belief in equal rights for all people, and *feminism*, which advocates for women's equal rights, to establish partnerships with communities for research purposes (Roysircar et al., 2019). The researcher can help focus group members assert their voice by taking the position of learner and allowing participants to teach them about an issue (Sherrif et al., 2014). For example, Perera et al. (2020) asked focus group participants to define the problems they faced as migrants or refugees. Focus group members discussed several pertinent issues, such as being bullied at school, as well as mental health issues, such as depression. As a result of the exhaustive description of problems, researchers were able to train volunteers about the full range of stated problems, as opposed to focusing on only a few issues.

By promoting authentic voice, focus group and interview data hold the potential to reflect the assertiveness of focus members and thus be perceived as authentic, or valid. Qualitative researchers strive to foster conditions that are conducive to authenticity in interviews and focus groups, such as trust, rapport, psychological safety, and the assurance of confidentiality. This is sometimes referred to as *trustworthiness*. If the information shared during an interview is obvious or shallow and lacks a clear and robust description, then the data are thought to be mediocre or as having poor validity. To help promote authentic voice in your research, ask yourself, "How will I allow for each participant to discuss as many issues as they wish that are relevant to each question?"

Step 3: Ensure Conceptual Heterogeneity

Because validity is the principal criterion of judging quality in data, researchers try to gather a full range of concepts with regard to the construct under investigation; that is, they endeavor to ensure *conceptual heterogeneity*. That means interview and focus group questions are key to spurring quality data. The aim of carefully worded and ordered protocols is to allow the person being interviewed to open up and express their thoughts. As a result, the researcher can gather a multitude of heterogeneous concepts pertaining to each topic explored in a focus group or interview. If simplistic, straightforward concepts are reported without nuance and thick description or without variations across interviewees, then readers may conclude that there is a lack of conceptual heterogeneity. This may cause them to question the validity of the interviews.

Step 4: Engage in Member-Checking

Member-checking can occur during the data collection phase, during data analysis, and/or as the results are written up. This means working with participants to determine whether they think the interview and focus group data are valid (Lincoln & Guba, 1985). In Chapter 3, I discussed how at the end of a focus group the moderator should paraphrase and summarize concepts that were discussed. Opening up dialogue about the concepts that were discussed allows participants to verify the concepts or correct and change the way a particular concept is characterized. Depending on the project and the researcher, it's also possible to provide participants with transcriptions and a brief write-up or report of the data that allows them to verify the presentation of the results. In interview studies, it's common for researchers to provide interview transcriptions to interviewees.

Step 5: Encourage Multivocality

Multivocality is the deliberate inclusion of multiple voices (Tracy, 2013). It is especially important when conducting focus groups, in which different or clashing perspectives might be offered on a topic, so, in addition to member-checking and ensuring the heterogeneity of concepts, interviewers and focus group moderators must also pay special attention to the representation of as many of the focus group members as possible. This is especially important for focus groups as opposed to interviews. Providing enough time for all members of a focus group to participate influences the development of the discussion and the range of topics discussed. Therefore, this principle is key to ensuring validity. Representation of these multiple, subjective voices in the analysis and results is important to reinforce credibility. In Chapter 3, I reviewed tactics for ensuring multiple voices are represented in a focus group.

Step 6: Use Triangulation and Crystallization

Triangulation (Jick, 1983) is a concept adapted from the field of air force control whereby three lines of sight are used to obtain the best estimate of a true location (Berg, 2004). The lines intersect to create a *triangle of error*, which contains the point at which the sight lines converge (Berg, 2004). In the social sciences, researchers use this approach to examine results across multiple informants or multiple sources of data to look for patterns as well as the possible confirmation of certain results. Each data source is examined with respect to another data source to evaluate its inherent validity.

Another term for triangulation is *convergent validation* (Campbell, 1956; Campbell & Fiske, 1959). The dimensions of time, space, and person are considered important aspects of triangulation in qualitative research (Denzin, 1978). For example, when triangulating interview or focus group data with observation data, the researcher can understand the social aspects of the study participants (Glaser & Strauss, 1967). There are many different ways to organize the comparison of data. Table 5.1 provides one suggested example for structuring triangulation across interview and focus group data by looking at themes. In each cell of the table, you could include either an illustrative quote or a rating of the robustness or salience of a theme's presence.

Table 5.1 is modifiable according to the type of data collected. For example, if you are conducting an interview-only study, you could modify the table to compare interviews. If you are conducting a mixed-methods study, you arguably could compare any type of data, as long as there are key ways to link them through themes. If the data do not relate, then triangulation across the sources may not be necessary or relevant to the research project.

Crystallization is a metaphor for considering the data as crystals that refract and thus cast various truths. It is another principle used in conjunction with triangulation (Richardson, 1994). The concept of crystallization complements triangulation because it highlights the complexities of each data source in addition to clarifying how the data compare or diverge when viewed in relationship to each other.

Table 5.1

Example Fill-In Table for Structuring Triangulation Across Interview and Focus Group Data

Theme	Interview A	Interview B	Notable interview similarities	Notable interview differences	Focus Group A	Focus Group B	Notable focus group similarities	Notable focus group differences	Comparison of interviews and focus groups
A									
Subtheme or code									
B									
Subtheme or code									
C									
Subtheme or code									

Researchers also use the principle of *comparison* (Maxwell, 2005) to draw out differences across interview and focus group data. For some studies, triangulation might mean examining multiple theories from the literature to compare and contrast them. In addition to these common uses of triangulation, perspectives across multiple researchers can help triangulate the interpretation of findings or results (see Step 10: Use Debriefing).

Step 7: Disclose Discrepant Information

Discrepant or contradictory information can be included to support validity. For instance, if perspectives or experiences described by participants appear contradictory, then it's important to acknowledge this in the reporting of the results. Doing so allows readers to trust that the researcher is not washing over, manipulating, or cherry-picking data to fit their research question or hypothesis; instead, disclosing discrepant information is a candid approach to showing the data in "true," or valid, form.

Step 8: Apply Lush, Thick Description

Lush description describes the quality and level of detail in qualitative writing (Tracy, 2013) that supports rigor and validity. It is also known as *thick description*. Applying the principle of lush, thick description to the writing process means offering a detailed and nuanced narrative picture of a certain feature of the study, mostly in the results section. Gilbert Ryle (1949) first coined the term "thick description" to refer to the challenge researchers face when attempting to depict the true complexity of perception and interpretation in social situations. Clifford Geertz (1973) expanded further on this concept to emphasize the importance of grasping and rendering narrative description in social science research (p. 10). The characterization of a situation, person, setting, or site not only helps bring research to life but also is the linchpin of validity. It shows the researcher's investment in attempting to be as valid as possible when describing unique features of the context of interviews and focus groups. McKenzie and Scheurich (2004) provided a lush, thick description of a theme called "Equity Trap 3: Avoidance and Employment of the Gaze," using an example from a dyadic interview with teachers. The following exchange between Tammie, a first-grade teacher, and Lauren, one of her coworkers, demonstrates the way that Lauren acquiesced when under the gaze of the other teachers:

> **Tammy:** It just irritates me to even think that it's me that has anything to do with their failure.
>
> **Lauren:** Maybe I'm an egomaniac, but I think teaching has everything to do with it. I really do think that. . . . And Tammy, you are selling, you are making yourself sound like a horrible [teacher] and you are not, you are a wonderful teacher.
>
> **Tammy:** No, that's what I'm saying, I am a good teacher, but if a student is a failure, that's not my fault. That's what I'm saying.
>
> **Lauren:** But if a student fails in your class, don't you feel, say a first-grader?
>
> **Tammy:** I feel like he [the student] got to me way too far behind, and I can't make up 3 years of difference in 1 year. I don't expect myself to be able to make up 3 years of difference in 1 year, and that doesn't make me a bad teacher.
>
> **Lauren:** That's a good way to put it.

In this exchange, even though Lauren first seemed appalled by Tammy's statements that her students' learning had nothing to do with her, she backed off and accepted Tammy's rationale that the students were just too far behind. . . . Thus, these teachers sought both to avoid the gaze of middle-class White parents, by moving from middle-class schools to low-income schools, and to deploy their own gaze to norm the thinking of any teacher who tried to assert an opposing view, especially one based on a positive view of the students or their parents. What is needed, then, as with the other equity traps, are strategies to undermine and remove this equity trap. (pp. 620–621)

Step 9: Engage in Continuous Data Saturation

Qualitative researchers should engage in *continuous data saturation,* as opposed to swooping in to analyze data in a piecemeal, or incomplete, fashion. Saturation connotes the process of soaking. Think of a sponge as a metaphor for the researcher soaking up data. This involves living with the data to understand them from the inside out, to gain a comprehensive understanding of them (Glaser & Strauss, 1967). In this way, validity, or accuracy, of data interpretation is ensured. Qualitative researchers must cultivate a trust in their own ability to know, reason, and interpret (Glaser & Strauss, 1967) data as part of the research process. Krefting (1991) referred to this as "establishing the authority of the researcher."

In addition to trust and knowledge-based authority, continuous data saturation includes the ability to adjust and readjust one's understanding of the data as an iterative process. For some research projects, this might mean adding additional interviews or focus groups to obtain more data over a prolonged period of time. Long-term research, including engaging participants over time, is considered a hallmark of qualitative validity (Krefting, 1991; Wolcott, 1999). Prolonged participation in a study is also a feature of validity.

Step 10: Use Debriefing

Debriefing straddles both validity and reliability. Although qualitative researchers are often referred to as the instrument in a project, and one may be the sole researcher or principal investigator, it is recommended that interviewers and focus group researchers confer with their peers about the nature of the data and results at special time points in the project. If the researcher is a student, this could mean discussing the data with a supervising professor to get feedback on decision-making points in the data collection and analysis process. In this way, the validity of the results is reinforced. In addition to validity, conferring with peer or expert researchers helps establish a discernible and thus reliable trail of how the research project has developed and changed (e.g., a thesis or dissertation project). Human subjects research often requires flexibility and adaptability on the part of the researcher in regard to the life context of the participants.

ANTICIPATING BARRIERS TO VALIDITY

With any good work, there are always hurdles and barriers. As researchers, we can anticipate and address the major barriers to establishing validity. Maxwell (2005) called these barriers to validity "threats," which is strong language but helpful in describing the importance of avoiding behaviors and data treatment practices that can impede the credibility of data interpretation. Instead of viewing these behaviors as looming external threats, try to see them as opportunities to learn how to improve your treatment and representation of qualitative data. Becoming aware of four particular pitfalls—perceived coercion, cherry-picking or selective anecdotalism, reductionism, and accurately transforming tabular data—can facilitate a smooth path to a rigorous, high-quality project. Conducting interviews and focus groups with these pitfalls in mind will help ensure that your research does not become vulnerable to criticism that might prevent your study from being approved by an institutional review board, a thesis committee, or an editorial or grant review committee.

Avoid Perceived Coercion

Integrity is paramount in social science research. Institutional review boards and national funding agencies do not approve and support research in which undue power, influence, or coercion is perceived to influence the relationship between researchers and participants. For example, if a teacher researches their students, then the barrier to validity is that the students might feel coerced to participate and provide only socially desirable and amicable interview or focus group responses to the teacher. Therefore, the students' responses would not necessarily be considered valid and authentic because they would not represent their actual thoughts. Thus, perceived coercion in interview and focus group recruitment is a possible barrier to validity. Conversely, lack of inclusion is also considered a problem. Providing equal opportunity to participate and revoke voluntary participation is important.

Be Cautious of Cherry-Picking or Selective Anecdotalism

Barriers to validity include *cherry-picking*, or selectively parsing data to analyze, leading to partial or incomplete results. *Selective anecdotalism* (Silverman & Marvasti, 2008) is the process of either describing a portion of the results without a sound rationale or taking the results out of context. Applying the principle of thick description, as described earlier, helps prevent selective anecdotalism because it frames the context of a theme and provides many details.

Be Aware of Reductionism

Very brief quotes from interviews or focus groups, as well as short descriptions of the research setting, can lead to *reductionism* (Bryman, 1988). When participant quotes and discussions are reduced, the data analysis appears insufficient or superficial, rendering the results incomplete and thus questionable. Again, reductionism implies a lack of thick description that is due to a harried or partial representation of the data. Qualitative researchers should look for signs that all the data have been treated in a comprehensive manner, without special attention to any specific portion. Rigid specification of data is considered a barrier to validity because it excludes the craft of interpretation (Wolcott, 1999). Therefore, writing a well-thought-out discussion section is important for avoiding reductionism and for elaborating on possible explanations when interpreting qualitative results (see Chapter 8 for tips on this).

Transforming Tabular Data Accurately

Qualitative data presented in chart or table form only, without sufficient analysis, can lead to misrepresentation of the results (Silverman & Marvasti, 2008). Researchers might organize the raw interview or focus group data in spreadsheets, but the data need to be transformed into codes and themes using appropriate data analytic techniques. For theses, dissertations, and program evaluations, presenting a summary of all data collected in table form in the method section can be helpful. The results section would then provide a thorough narrative description of the themes with exemplar quotes (this is discussed further in Chapter 6).

STEPS TO ADDRESS RELIABILITY

Have you ever played a team sport, and one of the players regularly came late to practice or missed part of a game? If so, your coach probably blew a fuse or simply chose not to put that player in the game very often. That's because that player wasn't being dependable, or reliable, when they were needed for the larger good of the team. They just couldn't get it together to arrive on time. In research, as in team sports, *reliability*—the process of using consistency and dependability in the overall research study as well as in smaller tasks, such as data analysis—helps ensure the success of the overall project. Not all researchers use the four reliability steps described in the following sections, at least not as systematically as they apply the validity steps. This is because validity and reliability are often contemplated in tandem, and each research project differs depending on the focus and types of data used.

Step 1: Strive for Consistency, Dependability, and Transparency

Reliable qualitative research depends on consistency, dependability, and transparency. How do you ensure that your work meets this standard? The first and most important thing you can do is keep records of research accessible—password protected and/or encrypted—to ensure they don't fall into the wrong hands. Research records include researcher notes; reflections and field notes; raw mp4 interview or focus group audio files; video files; data analysis codes; and consent forms, including human subjects forms. These records help the researcher organize data, especially when doing a thesis or dissertation. Well-organized records are key for locating, retrieving, identifying, and coding data (Hatch, 2002). Second, these records are important for storing and sharing data in a secure manner when participating on a team of researchers who might be located at various institutions and universities. Third, the records are important in the event that a study is audited. Examples of auditable data include human subjects protocol forms, such as consent and subject data. Grant-generated data from sponsored research projects may also include quarterly or annual reports to the funder, presentations, and manuscripts. Open verbal and written communication are hallmarks of quality social science research.

Step 2: Code Comprehensively

More detail about coding is provided in Chapter 6; for now, it's sufficient to note that comprehensively applying codes across data is an indicator of reliability. Researchers also should consider the degree to which the codes are faithfully and closely related to the transcriptions; this is also referred to as *structural coherence* (Krefting, 1991). Qualitative researchers must pay special attention to coding text exhaustively and applying codes in a reliable manner across texts. Before developing or switching to a new code, consider the degree to which each code is used in a comprehensive manner.

Step 3: Consider Interrater Reliability or Group Coding

Interrater reliability is a concept in quantitative research that refers to the degree to which a consensus or an agreement is calculated across two or more raters of the same material. In qualitative research, interrater reliability is not used universally. Some qualitative researchers do not think it is necessary to strive for convergence across multiple coders; however, many researchers advocate for discussing the codes in teams. Ambiguous or confusing excerpts can be viewed by multiple coders to see whether each coder arrives at a similar meaning. If the coders do not arrive at a similar meaning, this may be due to differences in interpretation, or it may be because the main researcher might see the excerpt in a different light as it relates to other parts of the interview. In that case, the researchers can discuss the various interpretations and arrive at a sound conclusion.

Step 4: Promote Transferability Over Generalizability

Generalizability, a common principle of quantitative research, refers to the degree to which results or outcomes can be predicted in other contexts. Qualitative researchers, though, do not see generalizability of their data as an end goal, at least not in the same way quantitative researchers do. In interviews and focus groups, depth over breadth is the focus. Likewise, qualitative researchers do not look for replicability in terms of strictly adhering to executing the same study in a new context to expect the same results; instead, they use the principle of transferability by looking for lessons learned from cases as potentially informative for other contexts or to yield policy implications (Lincoln & Guba, 1985; Yin, 2003). In this way, transferability is a carefully weighed decision on the part of the consumer of the research (Krueger & Casey, 2009). People reading and reviewing qualitative research might decide to use the results to try out a new curriculum or strategy, for example, in their own school or organization; however, they might not expect to duplicate results given the particularities of the study's context. Patton (2002) referred to this as "information-richness." That is why qualitative researchers focus on the inherent utility of research in and of itself and the implications for its use in other contexts over the principle of generalizability.

You can infuse your entire study with high standards of quality by adopting a proactive approach. To do this, spend some time considering the strategies listed in this chapter, and use them to develop checklists for yourself for each stage of the research project.

6

Transcribing and Coding

N ow that you have completed your interview or focus group, how do you transcribe and code the data you collected? If you're dreading this part, you're not alone! Researchers can suffer fatigue and burnout during coding. In my experience, this is partly because transcribing and coding happen in starts and fits, a bit like starting a car after the battery died: It might take several attempts to turn over the engine, but pretty soon it's humming along. To get in a rhythm with your transcriptions and coding, you'll need a plan for how to clean text, make text legible, and use appropriate notations. In Chapter 7, I provide more detail on qualitative data analysis methods.

Transcribing and coding go hand in hand. In the research cycle, they work well in tandem with each other, as opposed to being delayed, far apart from each other, or being broken into tasks by different researchers. It's often a mysterious process to novice researchers and for good reason. Not only are there many different methods, but also, in the past, qualitative

https://doi.org/10.1037/0000299-007
How to Interview and Conduct Focus Groups, by J. Katz-Buonincontro

research was often criticized for not providing clear and therefore replicable descriptions of coding methods. The general perception of qualitative analytic methods was that they seemed relativistic and indecipherable. As a result, unclear analytic methods can allow for cherry-picking, or bias in selecting which results to present. For that reason, the more recent trend in the social sciences, and psychological science in particular, is to be as open as possible and to explain the coding process in as much detail as allowed in a journal article, which has limited word counts.

This chapter walks you through the process of transcribing and coding. First, you'll learn six best practices for producing a clear transcription of interviews and focus groups that suits your research design and type of study participants. Next, you will learn six best practices for coding transcriptions. Learning these best practices will help prevent researcher burnout and fatigue, demystify the process, and provide strategies for enhancing the validity and reliability of your data.

TRANSCRIBING

Transcribing is the process of transforming audio or video files into typed text in order to subject the text to coding and further data analysis. In the past, researchers sometimes would just take notes during an interview or focus group instead of transcribing the data first, or they would just write up impressionistic notes of a conversation. Without a recording and a transcription, however, it is not possible to remember every part of what a person or a group of people say. Relying on memory means that important information might be excluded from coding as well as analysis, leading to incomplete and invalid research. As a result, using transcriptions as a crucial step of the data analytic process is now common practice.

It's also impossible to verify what people say in a transcription, especially if you need to report on the project's progress to an advisor or research team or if the project is audited. In addition, it's important to house transcription data in a secure manner on an encrypted computer for data security, which is a key requirement for human subjects research and institutions' policies on the responsible conduct of research.

Nowadays, researchers choose from three transcription tactics: (a) transcribe audio or video content themselves by playing files back and typing them up, (b) use automatic transcription if and when possible (e.g., artificial intelligence-based [AI] audio services that can be integrated with Zoom [https://zoom.us/] or other videoconferencing apps), or (c) have a professional transcription completed. Otter.ai (https://otter.ai/), for example, is a software company that partners with the Zoom online platform to provide secure, automatic transcription that can be saved to one's encrypted and authenticated hard drive or to the cloud. These transcriptions would still need to be reviewed, cleaned, and formatted.

Across these three approaches, the most important objective is to *account for a complete representation of the interview or focus group conversation in its entirety.* Complete, rather than partial, transcriptions help set you up for coding.

Transcribing interviews and focus group conversations is an excellent juncture in the research process at which to take stock of what the interviewee or focus group members discussed. Transcribing allows you as the researcher to reflect on the interview and check the degree to which your understanding of the interview corresponds to what was actually voiced and articulated. If this is your first time conducting an interview or a focus group, this reflective process prepares you to *memo*, or create short notes about the concepts being discussed in various passages of the transcription. This will also help you decide whether to plan for a follow-up interview or focus group.

The following sections describe six steps for handling the technical components of transcriptions.

Step 1: Play Back Audio Files to Develop the Gestalt, or Total Meaning, of an Interview or Focus Group

Playing and replaying the audio or video files of the interview or focus group will allow you the time and space to develop the *gestalt*, or total meaning, of the interview. This is important because your understanding of the interview or focus group may be fractured because it's likely you will be able to recall only sections or portions of what a person has voiced. A kaleidoscope is an apt metaphor for the process of understanding the many parts of what a person says. Each kaleidoscope crystal is a different shape and color, which represents the many facets of the conversation. Just as the kaleidoscope view changes with each rotation because of the combinations of the crystals, your memory of the interview can shift. That's because you were probably focused on keeping track of your interview questions or ensuring equal airtime when facilitating a focus group. Your job as the researcher is to transcribe the entirety of that interview so that the gestalt can be grasped, without the meanings constantly shifting.

Most likely you are eager to get through transcription to start coding. I hear you! Transcribing can be tedious work, even if you are just cleaning up an AI-generated transcript. Try not to rush through playbacks of the audio or video files when listening to them and typing. If you have interviewed several different people, your memory of the interviews can get choppy and sporadic. If you are working with a team and did not serve as the interviewer, consider playing back the audio files and just listening to them once through, before transcribing. This will orient you to the pacing and tone of the conversation as well as to potential distractions, such as background noise or idiosyncratic word pronunciations.

In Chapter 5, data saturation was discussed as a way of supporting validity. Data saturation may involve immersion on site as well as becoming familiar with data. If you develop a practice of listening to audio files, as described above, you can even clean your desk or organize your books while playing back the file. Or you can listen to the files while driving or walking the dog, for example. This helps you develop an understanding of the gestalt of the interview.

Playbacks will also allow you to unpack dense conversations or multiple speakers conversing. As we explored in previous chapters, focus groups are socially constructed speech acts. Understanding the ebb and flow between people also means understanding how the words they use represent their ideas. In addition to developing the gestalt of the interview, playing back the audio files allows you to hear yourself ask questions and reflect on this valuable communication skill, which was discussed in Chapter 2. Some people wince at the idea of hearing themselves talk or seeing themselves present. Nevertheless, you should focus on the cadence, demeanor, and flow of your questions. Consider how many pauses you used as well as any unnecessary "um"s. Note the reactions of the speaker and the way you connect with each interview. This will help you hone your interviewing skills for the next round of interviews.

For Step 1, ask yourself: "Am I accidentally cutting speakers off or not providing sufficient 'wait time' to let them flesh out their thoughts?" "With children and teens, does it sound as if I'm talking down to them?" "With so-called 'elite' interviewees who are known for their expertise or status in an organization, does it seem like I'm coming across as too tentative?"

Step 2: Format Your Transcription

Formatting each transcription helps prepare the text for coding. Most transcriptions use the entire page, but some transcriptions benefit from the creation of a table to separate line numbers, discussion, and codes or memos. It is helpful to add numbers to each line of the transcription. Add an extra line between speakers. You can refer to these line numbers when creating a codebook (see the Step 3: Create a Codebook section, later in this chapter) and selecting key quotes. Microsoft Word allows you to use special functions, such as Find/Replace, to help you save time, such as locating the name of the participant and replacing it with a pseudonym.

Notate who is speaking by using pseudonyms, numbers, or labels, such as "Interviewer" and "Interviewee A." In addition, experiment with differentiating the font of the speaker's text from that of the interviewer. For example, you might want to italicize the interviewee's response and boldface each question. You can use your word processor's "styles" function to establish a set font style for each speaker, eliminating the need to manually apply styles to each line or paragraph.

From there, you can italicize, boldface, highlight, or change the color of the font to emphasize certain passages. Be playful with this. As long as you don't change the words, or the order of the sentences, your formatting can help prepare the text for coding and making notes in the margins of the transcriptions. As I explained in Chapter 2, notes—called *memos*—are ways to offer your ideas on what you think the interviewee is saying or to comment on aspects such as the emotional valence of the passage.

Step 3: Provide Sentence-Level Clarity Without Compromising Authentic Voice

If you conducted the interview or focus group, as opposed to a colleague or research team member, then typing up an interview can be a valuable opportunity to listen to the interviewee or participant and make sure each point is represented in a clear way to prepare it for coding. As discussed earlier, you may also decide to use transcription software, use automatic transcription features, or pay for a professional transcription, or do a combination of both.

When playing back an audio file of an interview the first time, you might want to jot down some key time points, like 30 (minutes): 15 (seconds), to return to because they mark important points for coding. If you can type quickly, you might feel like it's easy to capture the main points; however, you might hear new details or shades of meaning when you come back through the recording. Speech tone, cadence, and speed vary considerably across people. This will affect your ability to understand what a person is saying and how to represent the points in text form.

Researchers often find themselves facing the dilemma of how to provide sentence-level clarity while preserving authentic voice in the transcription process. For example, you might feel pressure to erase or clean the transcriptions on the basis of the interviewee's style of speech. For example, Standing (1998) addressed issues of class representation in interviews with mothers who expressed interest in making their speech sound better or more professional. She argued that it is important to preserve their speech without reinforcing stereotypes of uneducated mothers. Therefore, I recommend spelling words and phrases as you hear them and allaying any stated concerns by describing the ethics of human subjects research to keep, not "massage," or change, raw data.

In addition to speech variation, it's important to review certain points to understand where to break speech into sentences. Thus, look for key pauses in speech to bracket the thoughts and determine where each sentence starts and stops. Oftentimes people speak in what seems like run-on thoughts. As a result, you will need to assign punctuation to each thought expressed. Align and couple the tone and emotional expression with the underlying thought. Some researchers, for example, denote crying with an asterisk (*; Kelly-Corless, 2020).

Step 4: Break Passages Into Smaller Units of Text

In addition to providing sentence-level clarity, passages of speech need to be broken down. How do we organize speech into smaller units of text? The way people speak can be haphazard and quite different from the way they write and organize their thoughts. Thus, consider ways to group sentences on a key topic into a paragraph. Later, this will help you figure out when a new concept is discussed, thereby signaling when to assign a new code. This also helps when sharing the transcription with another research team member. It's hard to read a paragraph that is an entire page in length, for example. To prevent coding burnout and fatigue, judiciously break passages into paragraphs or smaller units of text. As mentioned, a common practice is to assign numbers to each line in the transcription.

Prose Versus Stanza Layout

In addition to using a paragraph structure with numbered lines, consider breaking the text into even smaller units. For example, Reissman (2008, pp. 95–98) created two different transcripts based on the same interview. First, she used a traditional transcription:

01 *CR (Researcher)*: Go back a little bit in time-when [wife] left-you described
02 as bleak depression, very unhappy, tell me more about that.
03 *Rick*: I got a feeling that I'd never experienced before which is almost
04 a certain fran*t*icity-a *fran*tic feeling, I don't know what I'm going
05 to do, it almost like I was running right on the edge and I don't
06 know on the edge of *what-*

Notice how certain parts of a word, or a whole word, are italicized. Reissman described how she reflected on the meaning that started to emerge from the gestalt, or wholeness, of the interview. She struggled with how to break up the text. This is a clip of the next version of the transcript that she developed to emphasize the quality and types of emotions:

Affect
01 I got a feeling that   Stanza 1
02 I'd never experienced before
03 a certain *franticity*
04 *frantic* feeling
05 like I was running *right* on the edge   Stanza 2
06 and I don't know on the edge of *what*

Note the different arrangement of the same transcription. For Step 4, ask yourself, "How does the meaning of the interview segment change depending on the arrangement of the transcription passage?" and "How does the use of italics and number of stanzas affect the qualities of emotion in the transcription passage?"

Photographs, Artifacts, and Documents Accompanying Interviews

Drawings, photographs, and documents accompanying interviews can be clipped, digitized, and inserted into the passage of an interview in which the participant is discussing or referring to that item. Coupling the artifact with the interview passage allows for greater clarity in the coding process. The artifacts can be coded, in addition to the passage. Other materials might include musical instruments, maps, tools, plaques, religious texts, objects, unique landmarks, or pieces of technology—even garbage (Merriam, 2009)! Each work of art can be interpreted by the researcher in regard to how their meaning is associated with the meaning inherent in the interview. The researcher typically unpacks the relationship between the visual artifact and the other data in visual narratives (Reissman, 2008). For further reference to using the arts with interviews and focus groups, see Knowles and Cole's (2008) *Handbook of the Arts in Qualitative Research.*

Step 5: Seek Language Translations or Interpretation Assistance

In research projects in which the researcher does not speak the same language as the interviewee or focus group members, it is necessary to translate the native language of the participants into the language used by the researcher. Because cross-cultural qualitative research focuses on the choices made when transcribing interview data, the level of rigor when performing the translation is critical (Choi et al., 2012). The authenticity of the native language must be preserved to accurately convey experiences (Lopez et al., 2008). Translation competence in discourse and sociolinguistics (Squires, 2008) will affect the quality of the transcription, coding, and results, especially if the researcher would like to write up the results in the native language of the participants.

Language interpreters can also be used during the interview to help translate the native language of the speaker into the language in which the research will be published. If an interpreter is used, it's important that they do not alter, skip, or diminish the language and stories of the speakers. For example, certain words can generate multiple meanings, which implies selection of the meaning during the interpretation process (Lopez et al., 2008). Back-translation of the research language (e.g., English) to its original language can be an important step to establish the veracity of a speaker's meanings and intent (Brislin, 1970).

Step 6: Select a Notation System, and Adapt It as Needed

Transcriptions are full of the potential for uncovering gems you might not have noticed while conducting the interview or focus group. Be prepared to delight in finding surprise turns of phrase, emotion, and nuanced multimodal expression that go beyond recording the words. Adopt a notation system that represents and matches the type of expression in your transcription, and adapt it as needed to fit your speakers. For instance, if you interview people who use common acronyms, phrases, jokes, or terms, include those expressions, and ask them what they might mean.

Some interviews or focus groups include an activity such as live instruction, interactions between teams of students, improv theater, dancing, game playing, and so on. In such cases, it's important to develop a system for multimodal expression in the transcription to denote gestures and body movement. Mondada (2018) suggested, for videotaped interviews or focus groups, including a screenshot of a video or a photo and splicing it into the transcription to show direction of gaze and position of the body in relation to objects and other people. You can overlay names and/or arrows on the screenshot to emphasize the association between the lexical representation and the body movement. Certain methods exist for doing this that can be adapted for analyzing American Sign Language, for example (see Kita et al., 1997). Other approaches include tabular layouts to show multiple activities occurring simultaneously across time and space in a side-by-side format (Cowan, 2014). In this format, each column represents a separate activity, vocalization, gesture, or sound.

These are important opportunities to account for two aspects of transcriptions: (a) the action of each individual and (b) the reactions from other individuals. For these activities, it's especially important to review the audio or video multiple times to capture these nuances. Notations can be made in the sidebar of a transcription to comment on verbatim expressions such as "um"; gestures, such as rolling eyes; smiling; or laughter. *Naturalized transcription* does not eliminate speech utterances, no matter how seemingly small, precisely because they reveal the qualities of speech and conversation between people (Oliver et al., 2005). Examples of notations that can be included in naturalized transcription are provided in Table 6.1. A great way to make additional notes about interpreting these gestures is in a separate memo in which you describe interactions more fully and then hypothesize, or use conjecture about, the reasons and qualities for the expression and discuss your interpretation of the speaker's reactions.

Denaturalized transcription, by contrast, focuses on the basic meaning of the conversation, not the speech utterances. If you do not need detailed descriptions of how people talk, then you'd most likely use denaturalized transcription. When you feel uncertain of how to approach representation during and after transcription, consult with your team, your advisor, and/or your interviewees. This kind of consultation bolsters reflexivity used in research practice and reinforces the ethical resolution to such dilemmas.

Table 6.1	
Interview Notation Examples	
Notation	Example
(.)	Noticeable pause
(.3)	Pause time in tenths of seconds
.hh	Speaker's in-breath
hh	Speaker's out-breath
:	Stretching of preceding sound or letter
a	Speaker emphasis
.	Full stop or stopping fall in tone
((sniff))	Indicates a nonverbal activity
Wor-	Shows a sharp cutoff

Note. From "Constraints and Opportunities With Interview Transcription: Towards Reflection in Qualitative Research," by D. G. Oliver, J. M. Serovich, and T. L. Mason, 2005, *Social Forces, 84*(2), p. 1276 (https://doi.org/10.1353/sof.2006.0023). Copyright 2005 by Oxford University Press. Reprinted with permission.

With focus group transcriptions, you can use the same notations as in interview transcriptions. Unlike interview transcriptions, however, focus group transcriptions draw attention to the interaction of speech utterances across several persons. As a result, some notations may differ from interview notations. Notation examples you can use for focus group transcriptions are given in Table 6.2. Whether for interviews or focus groups, clear and detailed transcriptions set you up for coding.

CODING

Coding is the process of reviewing the transcriptions to determine what codes, or conceptual categories, can be identified in the text. Codes are the building blocks of your results. *Basic qualitative content analysis* is the act of partitioning audio- or video-based transcriptions into categories (Altheide, 1987; Strauss, 1990). In the coding process, each episode or instance of a verbal exchange is isolated and then described in terms of its smallest unit (Lincoln & Guba, 1985). These small units should be heuristic; that is, they should reveal and connect to the larger aim of the

Table 6.2	
Focus Group Notation Examples	
Category	Example
Laughing	Use (laughing) for one person; (laughter) for many people
Interruptions	Use a hyphen to indicate interruption(s), e.g., Let me-
Overlapping speech	Denote (overlapping) when people talk over each other
Garbled speech	If you can't understand what a person says, then indicate the garbled word in brackets [hello?]
Emphasis	Use capital letters for emphasis; YES!
Held sounds	Repeat letters to indicate long sounds, such as No-o-o-o-o
Paraphrasing others	Paraphrasing or mimicking others can be indicted with quotations or in parentheses: She said to me, "What?!" (sarcastic)

Note. From *Focus Group Methodology: Principles and Practice* (pp. 167–168), by P. Liamputtong, 2011, Sage Publications (https://doi.org/10.4135/9781473957657). Copyright 2011 by Sage Publications. Adapted with permission.

study (Lincoln & Guba, 1985). Once a small unit is identified, the researcher assigns a code: a word, term, or phrase that represents the unit. Assigning the codes in a consistent way helps ensure reliability in the coding process, as discussed in Chapter 5.

Now that you've painstakingly transcribed either interviews or focus groups using the six steps provided in the first half of this chapter, you're ready to code! To offer a metaphor, coding transcriptions is a little like walking into a meadow of freshly fallen snow. Like barren snow, clean transcription material is ready for you to mark up, notate, and code.

The sections that follow break down six concrete steps for coding that are common to qualitative research analysis strategies. The process you'll follow for coding is guided by four core principles: (a) *induction*, letting concepts emerge as close to their original meaning as possible; (b) *comparison*, defining concepts in relation to other concepts (Merriam, 2009); (c) *interpretation*, understanding the relationship of concepts to the research study aims, questions, and theory (Berg, 2004); and (d) *iteration*, the process of going through a cycle of inductive and deductive coding. Whereas induction constructs meaning from the small details in a bottom-up direction, deduction involves looking at the larger picture and identifying patterns from the top down.

In addition to written transcriptions, you can analyze other extant works using the coding process. These include works of art, videos, speeches, signage, maps, emails, blogs, and websites. Researchers can choose to code documents, images, and transcriptions by hand (e.g., by highlighting passages in different colors), or they may use basic document software (e.g., a spreadsheet).

Qualitative software analysis packages, such as NVivo (https://www. qsrinternational.com/) and Quirkos (https://www.quirkos.com/), are also available. These are sometimes referred to as CAQDAS: computer assisted qualitative data analysis software. The issue of assigning a code—which is a word or phrase—to the content still relies on the expertise of the individual researcher. That's why many qualitative researchers call the researcher the instrument. Exhibit 6.1 is a list of software commonly used to analyze transcriptions and extant documents such as websites, blogs, and texts. Now let's look at the six steps for coding.

Step 1: Differentiate Between Manifest Versus Latent Codes

When coding transcriptions, you'll notice obvious points being made versus more complex ones. *Manifest codes* are the more obvious points being made in text, whereas *latent codes* are considered to be the underpinning structure of a certain set of points (Berg, 2004). When sorting through a transcription, it's often easiest to start with codes that might seem obvious. One can use the Track Changes feature in Microsoft Word to highlight these points.

As you create memos to notate your reflections on the codes, you might reflect on more latent ideas in the transcription. Multiple reviews of transcriptions allow you to contemplate the many possible meanings in the text. Reviewing passages several times allows researchers to deepen their thinking about these latent structures and to make sure one is holistically applying codes. This process ensures *induction*; that is, letting the codes emerge as close to their original meaning.

Exhibit 6.1

List of Qualitative Software Packages

CAQDAS is a generic term for computer-assisted qualitative data analysis software. The following are examples of software packages. Please note that this is not an exhaustive list.

- NVivo (https://www.qsrinternational.com/): Coding software for qualitative and mixed-methods data
- MAXQDA (https://www.maxqda.com/): Qualitative coding software, including visual analyses, such as word clouds
- Dedoose (https://www.dedoose.com/): Qualitative coding software, including audio and visual data
- ATLAS.ti (https://atlasti.com/): Qualitative coding software, including media and surveys, with network visualization capabilities
- QDA Miner (https://provalisresearch.com/products/qualitative-data-analysis-software/): A text-mining tool focused on large amounts of word-based files, such as legal documents, in addition to other traditional qualitative data
- Word Stat (https://provalisresearch.com/products/content-analysis-software/): Text mining software
- Quirkos (https://www.quirkos.com/): Qualitative coding software to create and group themes that can be imported into SPSS for statistical analyses
- Raven's Eye (https://ravens-eye.net/): Cloud-based artificially intelligent natural language analysis tool, including language translation and transcription
- Discover Text (https://discovertext.com/): Focused on text, metadata, and social network analysis
- HyperRESEARCH (https://www.researchware.com/products/hyperresearch.html): Coding software with a relatively simple interface

Exhibit 6.1

List of Qualitative Software Packages (*Continued*)

- Transana (https://www.transana.com/): Relatively inexpensive coding software for longitudinal analyses
- V-Note (https://v-note.org/): Focused on video analysis and annotation
- Weft QDA (https://www.pressure.to/qda/): Open-source tool for analyzing test-based data
- f4analyse (https://www.audiotranskription.de): Simpler software, focused on transcription as well as coding

Step 2: Capture In Vivo Expressions and Interactions

As I mentioned earlier, coding is fun because interesting words and phrases pop up unexpectedly. *In vivo*, or "living," expressions document key turns of phrase or colloquial terms that capture the feeling or expressive qualities of the interview. Make note of in vivo terms associated with each code and notate the transcription number and page number to easily refer to them. Strauss (1990) described in vivo expressions as literal terms that are recorded verbatim from participants in an interview or focus group. The use of in vivo terms also supports validity. Researchers can pair an in vivo expression with a code to represent a sociological construct. For example, a participant might use the term "workaholic" to describe her orientation to her job. In a transcription passage, the researcher might develop a code on ways that scientists become obsessed with careers. Thus, the in vivo expression "workaholic" might be combined with the code "career obsession" to provide insight into a sociological phenomenon or construct (Berg, 2004). In vivo expressions paired with a code can help organize themes presented in the Results section; the terms can be subsumed under a heading, as in *"Workaholic:* career obsessions." In Chapter 8, I elaborate on the presentation of such a result.

Focus group coding can capture expressions as well as characterize interactions: common experiences, contradictions in the discussion, agreement, conflict, silenced viewpoints, or group alliances (Liamputtong, 2011). That's why notations are especially helpful during the transcription process.

Step 3: Create a Codebook

Think of codes as having plastic or molten qualities. Codes have structure, shape, and retention (integrity) but at the same time are moldable and pliable. With the possibility of codes changing and morphing as transcriptions are reviewed, how do we keep track, organize, and make sense out of our codes? Codebooks are a great way to accomplish this! Codebooks are extensive and comprehensive tables that allow us to not only list and describe the codes but also to revise, rewrite, and share codes across research partners.

Naming the Code

In the example codebook row shown in Table 6.3, the authors identify a code, define it, and relate it to an interviewee's experience. The code is then paired with a direct quote from the interview. Let's unpack this further: Notice that the code includes two important components: "perceived" and "burdensomeness" (instead of "burden"). These words are descriptors that were chosen carefully. The word "perceived" modifies the concept "burdensomeness" to signal to the reader that burdensomeness is a suite of representations identified by the interviewee. If it just stated "burden," then it would leave the reader wondering who derived the perception and what it was linked to. "Burdensomeness" is different from burden, which has several possible meanings, such as being a burden, feeling like a burden, and experiencing a burden. The suffix "-ness" implies a state, condition, quality, or degree of being a burden.

Defining the Code

Continuing with our example, "Perceived Burdensomeness" is defined as "the perception that one is incompetent or lacking self-efficacy." The

Table 6.3			
Example Codebook			
Code	Definition	Experiences	Example from interview
Perceived Burdensomeness	Perception that one is incompetent or lacking self-efficacy	Worthlessness	"Life is pointless. Like, if I'm not gonna be anything, like, I don't want to be just like another piece of scum on earth. I'd just rather die. I wouldn't have to wake up anymore, I wouldn't have to worry about how I'm gonna graduate from high school, what I have to do to get into a college, all the work, trying."

Note. Adapted from "Evaluating the Interpersonal-Psychological Theory of Suicide Among Latina Adolescents Using Qualitative Comparative Analysis," by L. E. Gulbas, C. Hausmann-Stabile, H. S. Szylk, and L. H. Zayas, 2019, *Qualitative Psychology, 6*(3), p. 302 (https://doi.org/10.1037/qup0000131). Copyright 2019 by the American Psychological Association.

definition is important because it allows you to remember it as you build the codebook with new codes. It's also great for keeping the definition clear for other collaborators so as to avoid confusion. In addition to the nuanced word choices of a code, also consider that the code might be worded differently if it were used in conjunction with a different type of data, such as a qualitative observation. If the code was used in conjunction with an observation, it might be worded as "Observed Burdensomeness." Therefore, "Perceived Burdensomeness" is suitable for interviews or focus groups because it connotes the perspective of the person voicing and describing the concept. This example also shows how the authors used the principle of interpretation to subsume a set of qualities or experiences under that concept, as expressed in the quote: ". . . worried feelings related to high school, college, life, and death." In this way, you as the coder can start to associate concepts. So, in Table 6.3 burdensomeness is affiliated with four concepts: high school, college, life, and death. In addition to naming and defining the code, some coders might add another column with a short label or abbreviation, such as "P.B. (Perceived Burdensomeness)."

In Vivo Quotes

In vivo quotes help explain what was said. This helps prepare you for writing up the results, so you can use the exemplar quote from the codebook. An *exemplar quote* is one that epitomizes the essence of that code. You may include several exemplar quotes in the last column of your codebook, but it is not necessary to include every quote related to that code in the codebook.

Step 4: Use an Iterative Coding Cycle

One of the biggest misconceptions of qualitative data analysis is that it relies solely on induction. This point has been debated by various qualitative scholars and mixed-methods researchers. Generally speaking, coding involves an iterative cycle that spans several phases: using inductive coding, creating a codebook, using deductive coding, and then combining both types of coding (see Figure 6.1).

Inductive coding is the process of grounding the codes in the data. Grounding codes in the data ensures that the codes are generative and emergent and thus authentic and valid. The word "inductive" comes from the Latin "in," or "towards," leading to a generalization. Inductive coding is performed a posteriori, or after the transcription is read and interpreted, as opposed to a priori, or before it is read. Codebooks are created using inductive codes. As mentioned earlier, the codes will shift and change.

Deductive coding is the process opposite to inductive coding: It involves applying previously created codes from the codebook or codes developed from the literature or from quantitative results (e.g., in a mixed-methods study). In Latin, "de" means "from," therefore directing or applying the code a priori, or first before the transcription is read. In a deductive approach you apply codes to data that have been collected or will be collected in the future, such as from more interviews or focus groups, or other types of data, such as observations.

Abductive coding is a combined process of using inductive codes while incorporating previously developed ones. Thus, you might switch from an inductive approach to a deductive approach and then back to an inductive approach.

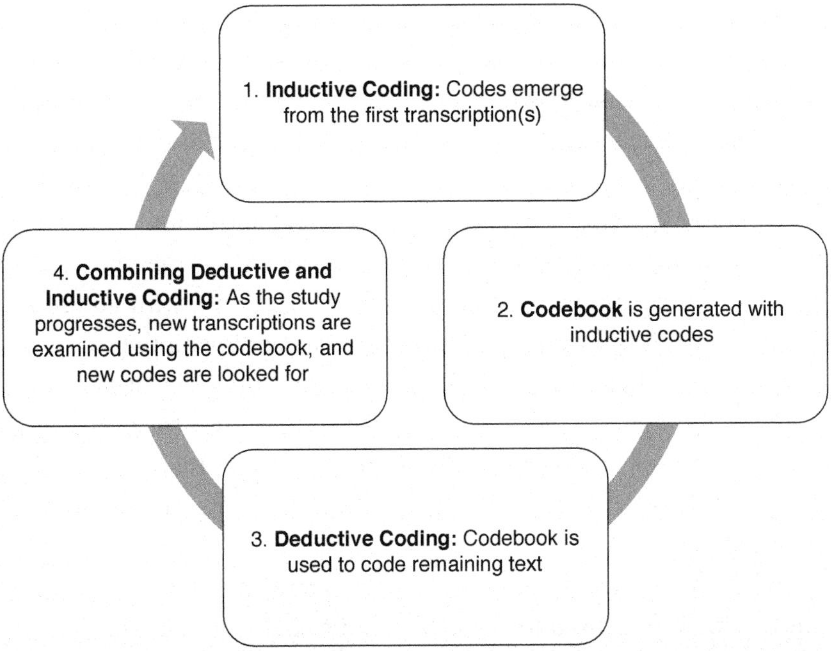

Figure 6.1

Iterative coding cycle.

Step 5: Develop Categories or Themes From Codes

After codes have been assigned across each passage of a transcription, the researcher can group the codes into categories, which are broader themes that span several codes. Some researchers refer to categories as *themes.* The most important tactic of grouping codes together in a category or by theme is *conceptual congruence,* which is an indicator of internal validity.

Depending on the approach they take, sometimes researchers create subcategories. Comparing categories with each other helps ensure distinctiveness. Categories shift throughout the process of coding because you'll most likely find yourself coding passages within one transcription as well as coding across transcriptions. Categories also continue to expand based on the principle of comparison: comparing and contrasting the meanings of the codes.

Category labels should remain somewhat fluid to truly capture the essence of the codes. Each category label should be mutually exclusive and describe the same level of abstraction (Merriam, 2009); that is, categories should offer similar levels of detail and reflect the data and research purpose.

Find the sweet spot between being general and being descriptive. A label such as "Beliefs" is too general. Beliefs about what? The label "Beliefs About Child Discipline" is more specific. Play around with additional detail to see if it is necessary. For example, depending on the study, the label "Parental Beliefs About Child Discipline" might be appropriate. However, if the study examines only parents, as opposed to multigenerational beliefs, then perhaps the description "parental" is an unnecessary detail. In this case, "Beliefs About Child Discipline" may be the best level of description.

Each subsequent label should reflect the same level of detail. As noted, this touches on the need for reliability in the coding process and consistency in research. Categories do not have to include the same number of codes. Some categories can include seven codes, whereas other categories might have only four to six codes, for example.

Step 6: Consider Collaborating With Multiple Coders

Using multiple coders helps defend the reliability of the code. Not every single transcription necessitates a full review by multiple coders. Some researchers select various passages to code collaboratively. The purpose of using multiple coders should be clarified across team members: to verify the nature of a code, to discuss latent structures, to clarify ambiguous or confusing passages, or to combat coding fatigue. It's okay if multiple coders do not initially agree on the application of every code. In fact, it's healthy to debate how to code certain passages. These debates should resolve in adding codes, changing a code, or the creation of new codes to adequately represent the interview or focus group.

Now that we've reviewed how the twin processes of transcription and coding get at the heart of analysis, it's time to build a case for what your collection of responses might mean. Beyond the basic content analysis described in this chapter, there are many additional types of coding. That's why Chapter 7 gives more detail on qualitative data analysis methods. In Chapter 7, I describe the five most common qualitative data analysis strategies: (a) grounded theory (Glaser & Strauss, 1967), (b) phenomenology (Giorgi, 1985; Moustakas, 1994), (c) ethnographic coding (Wolcott, 1999), (d) narrative analysis (Connelly & Clandinin, 1990; Polkinghorne, 1988; Reissman, 2008), and (e) case study analysis (Patton, 2002; Stake, 1995; Yin, 2003).

7

Analyzing Qualitative Data

Now that you have familiarized yourself with the basic coding process, you can examine some data analysis approaches that are unique to each of the five basic qualitative research designs introduced in Chapter 1 (i.e., ethnography, narrative analysis, phenomenology, grounded theory, and case study).

In this chapter, you'll learn to compare and contrast common data analysis strategies for ethnography, narrative analysis, phenomenology, grounded theory, and case study.

https://doi.org/10.1037/0000299-008
How to Interview and Conduct Focus Groups, by J. Katz-Buonincontro
Copyright © 2022 by the American Psychological Association. All rights reserved.

ETHNOGRAPHIC CODING

In Chapter 1, I discussed the suitability of ethnography to illuminating culture through identifying patterns of shared beliefs and identifies on the basis of group affiliations, histories, and backgrounds. Description, analysis, and interpretation are the main coding practices in ethnography.

Description

Description centers on the culture-sharing group's setting, events, or other important details in order for the reader to gain an *emic*, or insider, perspective. Researchers can also present the chronological unfolding of key events, such as a particular day, to describe the data. Wolcott (1999) described *progressive focusing* as a way to highlight key events or circumstances. Ethnographic accounts can range from more formalist descriptions to impressionistic ones (Van Maanen, 1982). Field notes are often included in addition to interview excerpts.

Analysis

Analysis of ethnographic data includes comparing individuals along the dimension of culture to highlight similarities and patterns. Subcultures are described in terms of the core values and shared beliefs. Diagrams, tables, and figures can be used to present the data.

Interpretation

Interpretation centers on comparing the analysis with larger theories. Ethnographers also provide descriptions of how the research affected them. This might include a further interpretation using a work of art, such as a poem (Creswell, 2007, 2008). Tropes (figures of speech), metaphors (symbols), or synecdoche (illustrations) are used to represent the data.

NARRATIVE ANALYSIS

Narrative analysis focuses typically on one person's life story as told through many interviews and interactions in the field. As such, the process of analysis incorporates fine-grained details such as gestures, sounds, and the dynamics of speech acts to fully capture and represent the biographical stories people tell. Narrative researchers consider both the personal and sociocultural dimensions of narratives. These narratives can become contested spaces for recounting and sometimes rejecting dominant narrative accounts in culture and in society. Narrative researchers often include an autobiographical component in the research report. This helps readers distinguish between the biographical account of the participant and the autobiographical account of the researcher, thus lending authenticity and validity. In contrast to case studies, the context and chronological order of events are ignored or underplayed (Reissman, 2008).

Compared with other forms of qualitative research, narrative analysis follows a diversity of forms and can be creative and flexible (Clandinin & Connelly, 2000). Narrative research is considered open to a range of techniques for performing analysis. For example, Reissman (2008) suggested four types: (a) thematic, (b) structural, (c) dialogic performance, and (d) visual. The property of time plays a huge role in describing narrative stories. And although there is no prescriptive or dominant strategy for narrative analysis, several scholars have described six main sections or passages that undergird many narrative analyses: (a) the abstract, (b) an orientation, (c) complicating action, (d) evaluation, (e) resolution, and (f) coda.

First, the *abstract* provides a summary of the narrative. An *orientation* helps readers develop a relationship to the narrative. Next, *complicating action* highlights an inconsistency or problem that arises and thus draws readers' attention to a specific dilemma or issue in the narrative. This can also be considered a key event or epiphany (Creswell, 2007). Denzin (1978) called this the *progressive-regressive method*, whereby an important anchoring event is described in terms of the participant before and after the event.

Evaluation is the narrator's interpretation of the complicating action. *Resolution* refers to a description of what happened in the narrative. In the *coda*, the researcher switches the focus from the past to the present. Coda sections focus on the current reality related to the biographical account. Metaphors are used to characterize how past experiences influence a person's contemporary life. For example, Angrosino (1989) used the metaphor of a bus ride to convey the journey of the person whose life is at the center of the narrative study.

PHENOMENOLOGY

Phenomenology examines the essence of lived experience by applying a four-stage analysis approach. Stories of lived experience are generated through multiple in-depth interviews: (a) epoche, (b) bracketing, (c) reduction, and (d) horizontalization. This essence is also called an *essential invariant structure* that characterizes what van Manen (1997) termed the "human lifeworld" centering on the "subjective inner life." The point of analysis is to make these lived experiences palpable to the readers.

Epoche

Epoche begins with self-examination: The researcher examines their own experiences and sets them aside in order to separate those experiences from those of the interviewee.

Bracketing

Bracketing is a reflexive process to prepare oneself to experience another person's experience during the interview process. For example, the researcher would make sure they have separation from the participant such that the researcher does not treat, educate, or take care of the participant. This allows the researcher to be open to and embrace, and thus begin to understand, another person's experience. The word "bracketing" was adopted from Husserl (1966/1991), who developed the term in mathematics to suspend belief and thus study the natural world (van Manen, 1997).

Reduction

Reduction centers on developing and clustering themes on the basis of significant passages of text. Important qualities are brought to life in the participant's subjective lifeworld. Honoring how we experience the world is an important aspect of phenomenology. Van Manen (1997) argued that it is impossible to understand our experiences as we undergo them and that we express our experiences only in a retrospective way.

Horizontalization

Horizontalization concludes the analysis process by attempting to see the experience from multiple viewpoints or roles. In some studies, phenomenological researchers also present an analysis of their own experiences. This autobiographical account serves to explain the relationship of the research to the researcher.

GROUNDED THEORY ANALYSIS: THE CONSTANT COMPARATIVE METHOD

In Chapter 1, grounded theory designs were explained as attempts to build a theory about stages and phases of how something occurs or unfolds. These designs are especially suitable for researching somatic (bodily) or emotional processes that involve liminal (transitional) states, phases, or other dynamic changes in a person's life that in turn affect states of being in the world and social processes. Grounded theorists develop psychological and sociological theoretical propositions anchored in data (including, but not limited to, interview data). Of the five general qualitative research approaches, the constant comparative method developed by Glaser and Strauss (1967) is known for its particularly iterative and immersive coding process.

In the constant comparison analysis method used with grounded theory designs, codes are referred to as *themes* or *dimensions*. In this book, however, I'll stick with a consistent use of the word "code" to mean the smallest unit of text identified by the researcher as having important or significant meaning. The constant comparative method is described in different ways depending on the specific reference, but it generally involves three phases: (a) open, (b) axial, and (c) selective coding (Strauss & Corbin, 1990).

Open Coding

Open coding is the process of exhaustively combing through text to fragment it into codes. Sometimes researchers use a guiding question to steer their open coding, such as, "How do participants characterize being homeless?" As a result, the researcher would generate codes that comprehensively describe the experience of homelessness as characterized by the participants, not necessarily by past studies. (The Discussion section might compare the experiences of the set of participants with those in past studies.) The researcher would then compare each example, or "incident," of that code. Hence, the coding is "comparative." In the process of comparison, the researcher is looking for the similarities of the codes across incidents within and across interviews.

Axial Coding

Axial coding is the process of integrating and linking open codes. The concept of axial coding is derived from the word "axis," or center, much like the spokes of the inside of a bicycle wheel radiate out from the center and overlap slightly as they touch the rim of the wheel. Axial coding brings together and subsumes open codes. The researcher looks for ways that aspects of various codes come together. In addition to other described processes, the dimension of time and representations of time according to participants' points of view are essential to fleshing out the way that codes interrelate.

Selective Coding

Selective coding is the process of further comparing data into even larger supercategories or themes that span the axial codes. This stage of coding, in which propositions and hypotheses are developed, is more abstract than the other stages. These form the core of grounded theory to help the researcher understand significant causal conditions, processes, strategies, and phenomena. While developing their selective coding scheme researchers often create a *conditional matrix*, a diagram that maps the relationships of these aspects (Creswell, 2007). Charmaz (2011) advocated for writing memos and using abductive reasoning to consider all possible theoretical explanations for social processes. This may include *theoretical sampling* to gather more interview or focus group data on the basis of what is being found in the data in terms of intermediate results.

CASE STUDY ANALYSIS

In contrast to narrative biographical stories, case studies emphasize the context of the individual as related to a social context or set of situations. Case studies examine units of analysis within a *bounded case* (Yin, 2003). Bounding the case is the process of focusing the scope of the case by delimiting the participants, events, locations, and groups. With a multiple case study design, similar cases are compared, and the cases are delimited in the same way. Therefore, if a mental health clinic is selected as a case, then a multiple case study design would compare and contrast the mental health clinic with other mental health clinics, as opposed to another type of case, such as a school, store, or community association. Clinic contexts such as geographical location, policies, and types of client or patient communities can vary.

Coding interviews as part of a comprehensive case study means comparing interview data with data from other sources, such as observation, reports, records, scores, or archival material. The principle of triangulation or corroboration is used when coding interviews and focus group data as compared to other data sources (see Chapter 5).

Because case studies are quite broad in terms of the types of data they yield, researchers recommend forming a database to ensure complete data collection. Case study databases help researchers identify any gaps, so they can shore up their data and prepare them for analysis.

In building the database, researchers typically proceed through the following steps of providing the site, establishing the site liaison, and identifying the people participating in the study and their contact information, as well as descriptions of the setting. Placing the case descriptions side by side allows one to draw out the nuanced differences across the cases.

Conducting Individual Case Analyses

Case studies can yield copious amounts of data, and therefore it is advisable to focus on an initial case or interview to start in-depth coding. Within-case analysis is followed by cross-case analysis. Communities as entities are described in the analysis (Yin, 2005). Thus, the locale and the unique case properties are brought to light using thick description (see Chapter 5).

Using Interview Codes to Then Code Other Data Sources

Codebooks from interviews can be used to code other types of data. In this way, the codes preserve a line of understanding across interviews, observations, and archival data, for example. This does not mean that new or emergent codes are ignored in other data, such as observations. Inconsistencies and gaps can be disclosed, discussed, and explained.

Conducting Cross-Case Comparative Analyses

A cross-case comparative analysis is performed in multiple case study designs. Larger themes account for variation across the cases. Thick description is used to eschew simplified representations of complex interactions in social contexts.

Taken together, these examples of data analyses developed over time within each qualitative research tradition will help you further clarify your options for analyzing your interview and focus group data in preparation for writing up the results. See Table 7.1. Don't forget to find some example published articles to help model the presentation of results and descriptions of the data analysis method. In Chapter 8, I'll walk you through various ways to organize and write up your results to disseminate your research to the wider research community.

Table 7.1

Qualitative Data Analysis Strategies

Qualitative paradigm	Purpose	Focus	Data analysis steps	Distinctive features
Ethnography	Authentically describe shared cultures through emic perspectives	Subcultures, values, and belief systems in the wider context of society	■ Description ■ Analysis ■ Interpretation	■ Progressive focusing ■ Pattern making ■ Inclusion of ethnographer's sense making ■ Field notes
Narrative	Anchor individual narrative stories around specific experiences and events	How individuals form stories and negotiate and contest larger meta-narratives	■ Abstract ■ Orientation ■ Complicating action ■ Evaluation ■ Resolution ■ Coda	■ In-depth life stories of one person
Phenomenology	Produce an understanding of the essence of human phenomena	Lived experiences of the human lifeworld	■ Epoche ■ Bracketing ■ Reduction ■ Horizontal-ization	■ Multiple interviews ■ Descriptions of subjective lifeworld ■ Essential lived experiences
Grounded theory	Create psychological or sociological theories of human experience	Liminal, somatic, or emotional experiences via time, conditions, and phases	Constant comparative coding: ■ Open ■ Axial ■ Selective	■ Theoretical sampling ■ Development of theoretical propositions ■ A conditional matrix
Case study	Illuminate the dimensions of a strategically selected case	Interactional, context bound, and situational (sometimes comparative)	■ Individual case analysis ■ Cross-case comparison	■ Compare various types of data ■ Link causes to outcomes ■ Produce examples and lessons learned for transferability

Writing Up and Publishing Results

Congratulations on completing your research study! I hope you are able to experience a newly found sense of accomplishment in realizing the dream laid out in your project's research design. This chapter is devoted to tips and strategies for writing up your research. Writing up and publishing results brings closure to the research cycle through dissemination of the results to a wider audience, whether it's a professor, a committee, a funder, a partner organization, or the academic community. The Discussion section of your paper builds on the results; compares them with those of previous studies; and suggests future steps for research, policy, and practice.

https://doi.org/10.1037/0000299-009
How to Interview and Conduct Focus Groups, by J. Katz-Buonincontro

In this chapter, you will learn steps to produce clear Results and Discussion sections of a published research report, such as a journal article. You will also learn strategies for converting a thesis, dissertation, or large grant project into six possible types of publications.

RESULTS SECTION

Compared with quantitative research, qualitative research Results sections are longer and use more diverse rhetorical conventions for presenting results. That's because there are so many qualitative method (and mixed-methods) paradigms, each of which dictates how to organize the presentation of the results. Conventions for composing results change over time, depending on shifts in methodological standards. For resources on current Journal Article Reporting Standards for qualitative and mixed-methods studies in the social sciences, see https://apastyle.apa.org/jars. The following sections discuss nine steps for writing strong, clear, and succinct Results sections.

Step 1: Write as You Research

Although results, or findings, are often written up after data have been collected and analyzed, you can start drafting preliminary results while data collection and analysis are still underway. The problem with waiting until the end of the study to write up results is that there are so many sections to compose and choices to make in regard to how to organize each section. Trying to write all the sections at once can be overwhelming. To prevent being overwhelmed, write up the Methods section and the literature review section before or as you collect data. For large research projects, create a simple outline for the Results section, too, and plug in bulleted points as you go. That way, writing up a thesis, dissertation, or journal article won't be as daunting.

Some people procrastinate or dread the writing process, whereas others relish the time required to bring the various parts of the project together in one integrated whole. You might enjoy writing together in a communal setting, using music to accompany the process, or seek alone time and space in quiet libraries. If you have engaged in collaborative analyses of interview or focus group data (Cornish et al., 2014), then this is a good time to decide who is responsible for writing each section of the paper. As I mentioned in Chapter 1, revisit agreements about authorship and order of authorship to acknowledge the contributions of each researcher because the scope and level of contributions change during the course of a project as well as during the writing process.

Step 2: Explore Rhetorical and Creative Conventions

Some scholars blend academic research with participatory or social justice work and hence push the boundaries of what is considered traditional scholarship. Although most qualitative research uses a traditional, detached tone for reporting results, some researchers prefer to use more impressionistic and emotional depictions of results (Tracy, 2013). Tenure and promotion guidelines at research universities often include a phrase called *creative activity* as evidence of research; this can refer to research presented as a work of art. Likewise, participation in social justice work may be an aim of your program, college, research assistantship, or grant project. For faculty, social justice work might fall under the "service to community" component of one's terms of employment, promotion, or tenure.

Some researchers use the arts to convey the meaning of the results and to leave a strong, lasting impact on the audience. Examples include storytelling, theatrical performances, poems, music, and works of art (e.g., collages). Art forms can be used to represent the results. For example, a researcher working with cancer patients might choose to publish results of the study conventionally, as an empirical research article, as well as disseminate songs that they created with participants about the experience of cancer. Visual narratives incorporate both a work of art as well as interview analysis (Reissman, 2008).

The arts can extend and deepen the social impact of research by making the findings more accessible and therefore easy to share with the general public. A few examples are showcasing songs in a live performance, exhibiting visual art installations in a gallery, publishing poems as a poetry collection, and using video diaries. All of these artistic options can be transcribed in addition to being presented. If you are interested in exploring these alternatives, check on the criteria of your grant, committee, program, or college or university. You might want to first publish your results in a journal article and then pursue the artistic options afterward.

Step 3: Organize the Results

Once you've decided what approach to take to present the results of your project, the next step is to organize your Results section. Provide an introductory paragraph that explains the organizational structure of the results. Example template language is, "The results from this phenomenological interview study are organized into four sections . . ." You would then proceed to explain how each section describes certain themes, such as "Teen parents' perspectives on educational attainment." Further options for organizing themes by research question or type of data, depending on the study design, are discussed next.

Organize by Research Question

Studies typically have at least two or more research questions or hypotheses. Therefore, you can opt to organize the results by each research question. This is especially helpful for committee members who will be reviewing a thesis or dissertation. Language you can use might be, "The first question addressed/concerned/examined . . ." You would then include the results and interview or focus group themes, grouped according to the first research question. You can continue using this structure by then discussing the second research question, followed by related themes, the third research question, followed by related themes, and so on. On occasion, student researchers might include a summary of responses organized by interview question; however, this convention is not used as much in empirical research articles because themes cut across interview questions.

Organize by Type of Data

If you have conducted a study that combines interviews with focus groups, as well as other types of data, you can choose to report the results separately for each type of data. In other words, delineate an Interview section that is distinct from a Focus Group section. If you are using interviews or focus groups in conjunction with survey or other quantitative data, then you would create a Qualitative Results section, further broken down by type of qualitative data. In this case, the Interview Results section would be a third-level heading. An example of these headings is provided in Exhibit 8.1.

Organize by Theme

Themes are informed not only by the codes but also by the qualitative paradigm used. In the case of a constructivist grounded theory focus group study aiming to identify conditions and phenomena, the researcher could directly reference grounded theory terms, such as "conditions" and "phenomena," in the theme headings. For example, Morrow and Smith (1995) examined constructions of survival and coping by women who survived childhood sexual abuse. Their Results section was organized into

---

Exhibit 8.1

Sample Organization of Results

Level 1: Results

Level 2: Qualitative Results (used only for mixed-methods presentation of results)

Level 3: Interviews

Level 4: Theme No. 1 and Quote(s)

Level 4: Theme No. 2, etc., and Quote(s)

Level 3: Focus Groups

Level 4: Theme No. 1 and Quote(s)

Level 4: Theme No. 2, etc., and Quote(s)

---

six main themes: (a) **Causal Conditions** (of Phenomena Related to Sexual Abuse), (b) **Phenomena** (Resulting From Cultural Norms and Forms of Sexual Abuse), (c) **Context** (in Which Survival and Coping Strategies Developed), (d) **Intervening Conditions** (Influencing Survival and Coping Strategies), (e) **Strategies** (for Surviving and Coping With Childhood Sexual Abuse), and (f) **Consequences** (of Strategies for Survival and Coping).

Organize by Profile or Case

Qualitative researchers focusing on a particular individual or case may wish to write up the results by profile or case. One way to do this is to construct a profile by copying and pasting sections of an interview transcription together (Seidman, 2013). This option makes it possible to examine data across multiple interviews with one person. Profiles provide a firsthand account of life experience, told in the first person. In addition, profiles allow the reader to bear witness to historical events and how they shape people's lives (Seidman, 2013, p. 127). Similar to crafting a profile, case descriptions provide a window into the everyday world of a group (Yin, 2005). Illustrative case studies describe daily interactions with special attention to particular instances, using pseudonyms for both names of organizations and persons. Tensions, problems, debates, or disagreements can be framed by providing thick descriptions of the history of the problem and the perspective of each party, group, or organization involved in the case study.

Organize by Theory or Construct

Qualitative research results can be presented in terms of how they support, extend, or disconfirm a prevalent theory or construct in a field. For example, the interview or focus group results might provide a window into how participants' experiences fall along a developmental continuum, stages of a disease, or an enculturation process. Gulbas et al. (2019) explained how Latina adolescents' experiences reflected various configurations of the interpersonal–psychological theory of suicide. The results did not present the participants as a monolithic group, however: Some participants expressed certain experiences, whereas others did not. In the end, the authors noted that not all the results aligned with the theory because of immigration and enculturation issues that affected each participant differently.

Step 4: Write Up Each Theme

Some qualitative research results unfold as first-person narration, from the stance or perspective of the interviewee, and sometimes the researcher is the source. There are many ways to approach reporting results in qualitative research, and many scholars adopt the strategy of reporting each theme on the basis of the coding process used. Drafting the results requires writing up the categories, or themes. It's up to you to decide which one to write up first. You can present each category or theme as an overarching heading and describe each code subsumed under it. This is where the codebook comes in handy! Include all the codes when writing up each theme, plus select quotes (see Step 5: Sample Exemplar Quotes section). Append the interview protocol or focus group guide separately, should space allow. Recall the principle of thick description (Geertz, 1973; Ryle, 1949) and lushness (Tracy, 2013) supported by exemplar quotes (see Chapter 5, this volume). When using a participatory analysis approach (Patton, 2002), you might need to discuss variations of interpretation across team members.

Step 5: Sample Exemplar Quotes

For each theme, there are many reasons to sample quotes, but what makes a quote exemplary? Make sure that the quote is tightly coupled with the theme description, rather than representing a small or random comment disassociated with the theme. The type of quote should exemplify the coherence to its parent theme in terms of "representativeness" (Pyrczak & Bruce, 1992). For example, if the theme is "Reasons for Dieting," selections such as "quotes expressing emotional reasons for dieting included . . ." could be used. As well, one could select quotes from male, female, and nonbinary persons and describe them as "quotes indicating gendered reasons for dieting."

Sometimes, small quotes are woven into the narrative, whereas larger block quotes are used to explain a theme. Use block quotes judiciously; that is, do not select quotes longer than three to five lines unless it is absolutely essential. In that case, consider whether longer quotes are used throughout the Results or just in one portion. Last, refrain from overreliance on quotes to describe the findings. Do not neglect your job as an analyst in providing insightful and succinct summaries of themes.

Step 6: Balance Theme Descriptions

It can be easy to get lost in the process of writing or carried away with describing an especially striking theme. After you compose each theme, examine the descriptions. Make sure they are balanced in terms of the quality of thick description used, the length of each description, and the way that quotes are used to exemplify the theme. If one theme has no quotes, but the other themes have long, richly detailed quotes, then the theme with no quotes will appear unsubstantiated, and the Results section will have less credibility.

Step 7: Illustrate Results With a Table or Figure

There are many ways to illustrate interview and focus group data. One of the easiest ways to organize a table is to refer to your codebook. Consider which codes and themes can be presented in a table. Then, read aloud the name of the theme and its description and possible quotes from the speakers. Are they clear and simply described? Refrain from wordy descriptions and descriptions that might require a second layer of interpretation on the part of readers. Readers should be able to read the table as a standalone presentation of data and refer to the Results section for further detail and context. Figures can illustrate the relationship of processes, contexts, and lived experiences that emerged from results. Figures are a good idea because text and tabular data alone often do not suffice for showing the fluid, interconnected nature of certain constructs. For more information on types of figures and which ones may be the best fit for the point you want to convey, see Chapter 7 of the *Publication Manual of the American Psychological Association* (American Psychological Association, 2020). Many qualitative data analysis software packages include options for displaying results as graphics; other design tools may be available to you through institutional subscriptions.

Step 8: Refrain From Direct Interpretation of the Results

This can be the trickiest part of writing up results. Report what people say, but be careful not to attribute certain motives, reasons, or justifications for *why* they say or feel a certain way. Even if you have training as a clinical psychologist, you will need to separate your role as a researcher from your training as a clinical psychologist. This ensures objectivity in the writing process. Stay true to the subjective perspectives of the individual or groups without interpreting, misconstruing, or distorting the meaning of their statements and stories. In the Discussion section you can offer suggestions for unpacking the results by comparing them with the results of other studies, as opposed to applying your own professional judgment.

Step 9: Summarize Themes

Qualitative Results sections are longer than quantitative Results sections; thus, be careful not to exceed the word count limit. If you do have space, one useful tip is to offer a brief summary of the themes before presenting the Discussion section. This helps provide an overview of all the themes before they are unpacked further.

DISCUSSION SECTION

Discussing the results, or findings, involves comparing the present study's results with those of earlier studies. Without a Discussion section, we wouldn't be able to understand the progression from one study to another.

In this way, the Discussion shows how a field takes shape by connecting the dots from one study to the next. With the six tips offered in the sections that follow, you can articulate how your particular research area extends previous studies and represents an advance across research over time.

Step 1: Summarize and Interpret Key Results

Interpretation is a key component of research (Wolcott, 1999). Making sense out of the results shows reflexivity. At the beginning of the Discussion section, summarize the key study results; then, unpack each of the results. To do this, you can describe each major contribution of the study under its own heading, subsumed under the main "Discussion" heading. For example, you can explicate connections across interviews and focus groups (Seidman, 2013).

Step 2: Describe Limitations

Every study—whether qualitative, quantitative, or mixed methods—has inherent limitations. Be sure to include a Limitations section, often subsumed under the main "Discussion" heading. Many researchers resort to stating a small sample size as a key limitation; however, depending on the study design this is not necessarily a drawback. Instead, discuss how various aspects of the research process, such as recruitment, study retention, and participant availability, may have influenced the study. In the Limitations section you also can disclose any bumps in the road, including ethical problems, language barriers, access to groups, or other ways that you feel your own bias may have affected the research.

Step 3: Address Shifts in Positionality and Alternative Explanations

Reflect on how your positionality has changed as a result of field engagement and what you learned from the study participants as well as the results. Offer alternative explanations as to specific details of the outcomes.

Use conditional language, such as "On the basis of the results, one possible explanation for the widespread phenomenon of dieting among (include certain population) is . . ." Try not to overinterpret or stray from the actual result.

Step 4: Compare Study Results With Those of Past Studies

As you organize each contribution of the study, compare the results with those of past studies. Cite the literature mentioned in the background section, or Chapter 2, of your thesis or dissertation. Provide a nuanced comparison that neither overstates the contribution of your study nor overstates the problems with past studies.

Step 5: Elucidate Contribution to Theory

Theory may seem intimidating, but many studies offer useful frameworks for combining theories or using existing theories in new contexts or fields (i.e., interdisciplinary or transdisciplinary work). Clearly state how the study might contribute to a certain theory as described in the theoretical framework and literature review. If you did not discuss a theory leading up to the Methods section, then do not mention and refer to it for the first time in the Discussion section.

Step 6: Articulate Transferability and Recommendations for Policy and Practice

Transferability is the concept of using research results gleaned from a study to a real-life situation (Lincoln & Guba, 1985). You can discuss how the results may or may not transfer to another setting. This allows, and in fact empowers, the readers to make judgments about using the results in a new context. The principle of transferability, or *naturalistic generalization* (Stake, 2000), is not to assume that all results can be replicated and applied elsewhere; instead, it creates a conversation to consider the appropriateness of using the results in what researchers call "local conditions" (Cronbach, 1975).

In addition, it's important to offer concrete implications or recommendations for policy or practice, without straying from the study's results. Miles and Huberman (1994) advocated for usable knowledge to guide action, grounded in ethical issues and considerations. Practical implications can be used for improving the design and offering of interventions, programs, workshops, classes, and trainings. Clinicians, faculty members, teachers, administrators, and human resources and professional development staff in particular look for research that is usable, applicable, and research based. For example, Henderson et al.'s (2020) "Implications" section advocates for adults to acknowledge their vulnerability so as to counter racism in schools and use emancipatory strategies to help Black youth.

Some journals seek bulleted recommendations for practice at the conclusion of a research article. Most articles provide a concluding statement or paragraph that offers an even briefer summary of key results combined with suggested future work. These statements provide a key takeaway that has a neutral yet forward-facing tone.

PUBLISHING YOUR WORK

Publishing can feel daunting, especially if it's the first time you've published interview or focus group data. However, the trend in academia is to publish more student research and to provide online open-source journals to expedite the publishing process. These trends bode well for those interested in disseminating research results. Federal funding agencies and foundations also like to know that their dollars are well spent by bridging academia with the process of knowledge dissemination and the potential to affect society (National Science Foundation, 2021). With this in mind, you can feel confident following the steps listed next so that others can read your work.

Step 1: Convert a Project, Thesis, or Dissertation Into a Publication

Many students aim to convert an independent research project, thesis, or dissertation into a publication. Sometimes this can be straightforward;

other times several steps are required to convert a smaller part of a larger thesis or dissertation into a publication. Therefore, your first step is to consider how to focus a discrete part of a multipronged project into a clear, focused manuscript. Because there are many choices for focusing a paper, contemplate which part or parts can be included in the manuscript. Grants often require yearly reports, which vary according to the specific funder. For grant reporting guidelines, refer to the funder and their examples. The next paragraphs suggest some ideas for how you can convert your project into six different types of publications.

Literature Reviews

A literature review manuscript can expand effectively on a Chapter 2/ literature review section of a thesis or dissertation to create a full-blown article. After all, literature reviews require a lot of time, especially if they are *systematic*, meaning you have scoured databases using search terms within designated time periods. Some students adopt the opposite strategy: They prepare a literature review manuscript in preparation for writing Chapter 2. Such papers include a Methods section to clarify which databases were used, how studies were selected, the sample size of the studies, and the process of synthesizing and analyzing those studies. As such, literature reviews can produce wonderful landscapes on key topics, which can be extremely beneficial to other students and those interested in your research area. In addition to literature reviews, qualitative meta-analyses involve gathering and summarizing results from studies to show patterns and gaps.

Empirical Articles

The gold standard of academic publishing is the empirical research article. Standard empirical manuscripts include the essential elements of each thesis or dissertation chapter. However, if you have a thesis or dissertation that is 100 or more pages, condense only the key elements of each chapter. Be sure to balance each section. Helpful references as you create your article include the American Psychological Association's (2020) *Publication Manual* and Levitt's (2020) book, *Reporting Qualitative Research in Psychology*.

Methods Articles

Methods articles discuss innovative ways of using a method in a certain context. They explore specific nuances of and challenges to conducting interviews and focus groups. For example, a methods article could discuss the development of a partnership between a research team and a community or school district through culturally responsive focus groups. Another example could be changing methods midstream in a project, such as transforming a traditional classroom research project into a participatory action research one, to allow for the voices of multiple youth groups. The article perhaps could focus on working with youth to learn how to interview, describing what the researcher and the youth learned and why it is important for social justice awareness and activism.

Conceptual Articles

Conceptual articles propagate new theories or illustrate the integration of concepts to initiate a new line of research. One example might be an article that addresses how to conduct research on a digital game, using a historical overview of related research and suggesting a new research agenda that incorporates cognitive psychology to design digital gaming principles and identify their effects on game players. The article would outline theoretical principles that guided the research process and collaborations across disciplines such as psychology, education, computer science, and technology teachers in a local school district, for example.

Practitioner Articles

Practitioner articles discuss the practicalities of using a certain clinical, teaching, or training method. They are geared toward impact, use, and application. For example, a practitioner article could discuss professional development issues as part of a larger research project that used interviews or focus groups. Professional development designs could be described and then contrasted with those of similar designs in certain fields. In addition, a practitioner article might translate research from an area into practice.

Chapters

Writing a chapter for books and handbooks typically involves summarizing part of a research project or synthesizing information across several research projects, then relating that material to the overall book topic. Books can be quite specialized, and for that reason there are two ways chapters are solicited. First, the editor might preselect the potential authors. Alternatively, an editor might place a call inviting submissions for peer review, which can be found through listservs or ads placed at the back of journals, in newsletters, or on websites.

During the writing process, beware of creating a "Frankenstein" paper that pieces together incompatible parts of your original project. For instance, if you worked on a large project that had a social–emotional component, an academic component, and a health component, consider isolating each of these parts into separate chapters. Alternatively, if the aim is to examine a relationship across some or all of the study components, then perhaps the chapter can focus on pilot data (initial or exploratory) or narrow the focus to the group, classroom, or clinic level (case study approach). A second consideration for narrowing the focus of a chapter is using a journal's criteria, such as word count.

Step 2: Identify and Compare Journals in Qualitative Research

Now that you've considered which type of publication to craft, it's time to identify and compare various journals in your specific field as well as in qualitative research overall. Several journals are devoted to qualitative research studies, but they differ in their standards and audience. Table 8.1 lists some qualitative journals and their publishers.

Step 3: Consider the Journal's Focus

In addition to identifying journals, be sure to match your study to the aims and scope of each journal beyond the general area of "qualitative research." You may wish to consider journals that publish in your home discipline or special domain. If you are combining interview and focus group data

Table 8.1

Example Qualitative Journals

Journal	Publisher
Qualitative Psychology	American Psychological Association
International Journal of Qualitative Methods	SAGE Journals
Qualitative Research	SAGE Journals
Qualitative Health Research	SAGE Journals
Qualitative Inquiry	SAGE Journals
The Qualitative Report	Halmos College of Arts and Sciences, Nova Southeastern University
International Journal of Qualitative Studies on Health and Well-Being	Taylor & Francis
Qualitative Sociology	Springer
Journal of Contemporary Ethnography	SAGE Journals
Qualitative Research in Health	Elsevier
Qualitative Social Work	SAGE Journals
Qualitative Research Reports in Communication	Taylor & Francis
Narrative Inquiry in Bioethics: A Journal of Qualitative Research	Johns Hopkins University Press
Qualitative Marketing Research	SAGE Publications
Qualitative Research in Psychology	Taylor & Francis
Qualitative Research in Medicine & Healthcare	Page Press
Qualitative Research Journal	Emerald Insight
International Journal of Qualitative Studies in Education	Taylor & Francis
American Journal of Qualitative Research	Center for Ethnic and Cultural Studies in Fort Myers, Florida, United States
Qualitative Research in Education	Hipatia Press
Global Qualitative Nursing Research	SAGE Journals
International Review of Qualitative Research	SAGE Journals
Qualitative Research in Organizations and Management	Emerald Insight
Forum: Qualitative Social Research	Institut für Qualitative Forschung, Internationale Akademie Berlin, Germany

Table 8.1

Example Qualitative Journals (*Continued*)

Journal	Publisher
International Journal of Qualitative Research in Services	InderScience
Journal of Ethnographic & Qualitative Research	Rotating universities
Qualitative Sociology Review	University of Łódź, Łódź, Poland
Departures in Critical Qualitative Research	University of California Press
New School Psychology Bulletin	The New School, New York

with quantitative data, you can consider mixed-methods journals. Because there are many qualitative and mixed-methods designs, it is beneficial to do a library database search and find published articles in the journal you wish to publish in that use designs that are identical or similar to yours. Cite those articles to support your design and analysis choices, in addition to citing seminal qualitative articles, chapters, and books.

Step 4: Find Articles Related to Your Design or Analysis

You may also want to find exemplars of published articles of research that used the same or similar type of qualitative data analysis. This can guide you as to the level of detail needed for explaining the design, data collection, and analysis approach. Many editorial review boards are looking for serious student researchers to volunteer and serve as student reviewers. This is a great way to become familiar with quality journals in which you'd like to publish. Also, if you decide to go into academia, you can serve as an official reviewer. Eventually, you may even want to apply to be an associate editor, managing editor, or overall editor of that journal or another journal in which you've published.

When writing up your results and considering the various formats for publishing your work, imagining how readers will engage with the data is helpful. What interview stories really stick out in your mind, and what makes them fascinating? How can you bring these stories and perspectives to life through your writing, even if they might be controversial or a bit adversarial (e.g., differing views in a small group interview)? If this is hard to picture, try to imagine yourself discussing your work with a friend or your faculty dissertation committee. What questions will they likely ask you, and how will you respond? Alternatively, imagine yourself presenting to audience members at a conference. Which points will really grab their attention and get them scrambling to take notes? For ideas on presenting in ways that will engage, consider looking at researchers' social media pages or following hashtags from events at which scientists are presenting original work. How do they build up to each post- or comment-worthy point, and how does their audience respond? Anticipating this back-and-forth exchange can help you infuse your writing with energy. It can also help you prepare to answer questions about your work—and perhaps even envision future directions for your career as a researcher.

Conclusion

Truth is so rare, it is delightful to tell it.

—Emily Dickinson

Why are words powerful? As the poet Emily Dickinson implies, words convey *truth*. Researchers would say interviews convey *multiple truths*. Talking about real experiences, views, and feelings is at the heart of interviews. Although our truths are not always "delightful," researchers can help people share them by telling their stories. As the quote also suggests, truth can be *rare*. That's why interviews are one of the most powerful ways to investigate stories that are *rarely* told.

With care not to romanticize or essentialize others' personal stories, qualitative researchers discern conditions, patterns, and themes within and across interviews. Such research can reveal the racism in which certain scientific assumptions are grounded, for example (Du Bois, 1896/1967).

https://doi.org/10.1037/0000299-010
How to Interview and Conduct Focus Groups, by J. Katz-Buonincontro
Copyright © 2022 by the American Psychological Association. All rights reserved.

It can bring to light the voices of minoritized people, such as homeless youth (Toolis & Hammack, 2015) or migrants (Esposito et al., 2019). It can also unpack complex intersectional issues, such as privilege, gender, race, and oppression within different people's experience of sexual objectification, for example (Flores et al., 2018). These stories might otherwise go untold, be covered up, or simply left unknown in the world.

By conducting interview and focus group research you can be part of the research community that helps the larger public understand the nuances of humanity's lived experience. Some researchers believe that interviews can help promulgate truth and in doing so be used for important purposes such as improving living conditions, educational access, and other social justice issues. Reading research helps us learn about people, develop empathy, break through isolation from different communities, and motivate us to take action to improve the world.

I won't deny that conducting interviews and focus groups can be a little challenging at first, and oftentimes it is very challenging, but I've also found it to be immensely rewarding in the end. When your data set is made up of narratives, your brain commits them to memory more readily. Long after your study has been published, you'll likely recall fascinating stories, debates, and discussions in a visceral way. Through interviewing strangers, you'll learn how to empathize and connect with people in your daily circles and perhaps even find new ways of framing your disagreements.

If you enjoy this type of data collection, your hard work and enjoyment will shine through. I invite you to use, share, and adapt this book's many tables, checklists, examples, and resources for building your own research toolkit. Who knows, maybe someday your research will change the world! And in the words of Emily Dickinson, you'll find "delight" in doing so.

Appendix A:
Summary of Action Steps

CHAPTER 2: INTERVIEWING

Step	What does it involve?	How will the step help my research?
1: Provide a Rationale for Selecting Interview Methods	Describe how you will access people's innermost thoughts, feelings, beliefs, opinions, and/or experiences	Shows how other data gained from surveys and observations cannot access human thought like interviews can
2: Select a Sampling Method	Clarify the best fit of either convenience, maximal variation sampling, purposive/purposeful, snowball, quota, community nomination sampling	Tailors the sampling method to your research design and research questions
3: Choose a Qualitative Design and Orientation	Choose among ethnographic, phenomenological, narrative, grounded theory, case study, or other designs	Focuses the interview and the interview questions
4: Find Published Exemplars of Interview Studies	Compare and contrast interview approaches	Provides a precedent for applying the interview method to your research topic

(continues)

Step	What does it involve?	How will the step help my research?
5: Select an Interview Type	Design the interview as unstructured, semistructured, dialogic, dyadic, structured, or photo/art elicitation	Shapes the interview protocol, prepares for the use of appropriate technology (online platform)
6: Draft an Interview Protocol	Construct the most essential, burning questions	Links the interview questions back to the research purpose and the research questions
7: Pilot-Test the Interview Protocol	Practice interviewing	Omits confusing and two-tailed questions
8: Submit a Human Subjects Protocol, Including Consent Forms	Obtain permission to conduct research	Demonstrates training in responsible conduct of research
9: Recruit Interviewees and Obtain Consent From Them	Ensure voluntary consent without coercion	Guarantees confidentiality and anonymity
10: Cultivate Rapport and Trust During the Interview	Empower interviewees	Allows people to disclose authentic thoughts, thus supporting validity of the research project
11: Record the Interview	Provide a record for transcription and/or translation	Enables you to upload the transcriptions to a qualitative coding software program
12: Take Notes and Memos	Remember what people are saying during (and after) the interview	Prepares for coding by helping you identify emergent themes

CHAPTER 3: CONDUCTING FOCUS GROUPS

Step	What does it involve?	How will the step help my research?
1: Clarify the Focus Group Purpose and Orientation	Decide why a focus group is more suitable than an interview	Plans for either bracketing, creating a touchstone, or using an extended focus group
2: Select a Homogeneous Grouping Characteristic	Figure out how to group people on the basis of a key similarity	Determines how many focus groups are appropriate for the research topic
3: Designate a Moderator	Find a moderator, preferably one with insider status, so you can observe the focus group, take notes, and understand the discussion	Provides more objectivity
4: Develop a Focus Group Guide	Provide structure, guidelines, and consistency for the moderator across focus groups	Supports reliability
5: Develop a Group Agreement for Maintaining Confidentiality	Help focus group members feel comfortable, respecting each perspective and helping them feel free to talk	Enhances research credibility and professionalism
6: Use Effective Facilitation Principles	Allow for psychological safety, mutual respect, equal air time, and heterogeneity of thought	Supports authenticity/validity
7: Set Up the Focus Group Room	Prepare the logistics for the focus group and anticipate the needs of the focus group members	Includes recording for transcription purposes
8: Conduct the Focus Group	Use a welcoming tone, encourage participation from all people, allow for distress, and so on	Using best practices will enhance credibility of project for recruiting additional focus group participants

CHAPTER 5: ENHANCING RIGOR, AUTHENTICITY, AND VALIDITY

Step	What does it involve?	How will the step help my research?
1: Describe the Researcher's Identity and Positionality	■ Reflect on and discuss your assumptions and preconceived ideas ■ Provide a narrative statement on your own power, privilege, and identity	Builds relational trust with research participants
2: Promote Authentic Voice	Empower interviewees and focus group members to assert their voice	Supports validity
3: Ensure Conceptual Heterogeneity	■ Gather a multitude of different points of view ■ Ensure a range of concepts are discussed and described	Broadens data points
4: Engage in Member-Checking	Get feedback from interviewees on transcriptions	Confirms accuracy of written representation of data
5: Encourage Multivocality	Allow all participants to speak and express their views	Provides differing or clashing viewpoints
6: Use Triangulation and Crystallization	■ Compare data sets ■ Examine results from more than one theory ■ Gather multiple researcher perspectives during coding, analysis, and interpretation phases	Reveals areas of convergence and divergence within and across data
7: Disclose Discrepant Information	Include, rather than omit, any contradictory data	Shows any possible gaps; enhances transparency
8: Apply Lush, Thick Description	Elaborate on details	Contextualizes data
9: Engage in Continuous Data Saturation	Be thorough (e.g., multiple interviews with an individual, interviews with a purposive sample of participants, multiple focus groups)	Allows for adjusting and readjusting your understanding of the data
10: Use Debriefing	Consult with peers about the data	Reinforces validity; creates a traceable trail of changes to the project

CHAPTER 5: ADDRESSING RELIABILITY

Step	What does it involve?	How will the step help my research?
1: Strive for Consistency, Dependability, and Transparency	■ Keep records accessible and protect data ■ Use notes, memos, and tables to track interviews and metadata such as time, date, location of interview, and completion of consent forms	Ensures data security and transparency of the process
2: Code Comprehensively	■ Cover transcriptions in their entirety ■ Connect codes closely to the raw data	Uncovers themes
3: Consider Interrater Reliability or Group Coding	■ Provide various interpretations of the data ■ Examine the degree of consensus in the coding process	■ Shows consistency in the data analysis process ■ Ensures diversity and different cultural interpretations
4: Promote Transferability Over Generalizability	■ Show connections between contexts rather than implying prediction ■ Look at the potential for using the results to inform or shape policy, procedures, or treatments	■ Demonstrates a wider relevance to the field ■ Allows you to consider adjustments that might be needed for application of the results in new contexts

CHAPTER 6: TRANSCRIBING

Step	What does it involve?	How will the step help my research?
1: Play Back Audio Files to Develop the Gestalt, or Total Meaning, of an Interview or Focus Group	■ Catch what you might have missed when conducting the interview or focus group ■ Improve your communication skills for the next interview or focus group	Supports data saturation, a validity strategy
2: Format Your Transcription	Notate and format the passages of text	Provides traceable records of the interview or focus group
3: Provide Sentence-Level Clarity Without Compromising Authentic Voice	Figure out where one point starts and stops	Organizes the transcription
4: Break Passages Into Smaller Units of Text	Play with the structure of prose versus stanza	Emphasizes different meanings to relate back to your research questions
5: Seek Language Translations or Interpretation Assistance	When needed, keep interpretation and translation data as close as possible to the original voices of the participants	Enhances validity
6: Select a Notation System and Adapt It as Needed	Choose from naturalized or denaturalized transcription	For focus groups, emphasizes differences across people and focus groups

CHAPTER 6: CODING

Step	Why do I need the step?	How will the step help my research?
1: Differentiate Between Manifest Versus Latent Codes	Figure out obvious versus less obvious points	Marks up areas that will need additional review
2: Capture In Vivo Expressions and Interactions	Exemplar quotes can be paired with a code in the codebook	Enhances validity and helps organize themes in the Results section
3: Create a Codebook	Name and define codes coupled with in vivo quotes	Organizes the codes for sharing with multiple raters and for presenting data in research presentations, conferences, and manuscripts
4: Use an Iterative Coding Cycle	Go through the full cycle of inductive (emergent), deductive (applied to transcriptions), and abductive (both) coding	Supports thorough and consistent coding practices
5: Develop Categories or Themes From Codes	Use categories or themes to cluster codes according to their conceptual congruence	Prepares for writing up the results
6: Consider Collaborating With Multiple Coders	Choose from interrater reliability to achieve a consensus or multiple raters to allow for multiple interpretations	Ensures reliability

CHAPTER 8: WRITING UP RESULTS

Step	What does it involve?	How will the step help my research?
1: Write as You Research	■ Write up the Methods section and the literature section before or as you collect data ■ Create a simple outline, and plug in bulleted points as you go	■ Stays true to the actual processes of each research stage, which supports validity and reliability ■ Prevents feelings of being overwhelmed by having to write up everything at the end of a project
2: Explore Rhetorical and Creative Conventions	Whether traditional, community, social justice, or arts oriented, find a style that fits your voice as a researcher as well as the requirements of your job, program, or grant	Extends and deepens the social impact of your research
3: Organize the Results	Organize the results by research question, type of data, theme, profile or case, theory, or construct	Helps readers understand the results and helps the manuscript get published
4: Write Up Each Theme	Use the codebook to provide lush, thick description of themes	Supports authenticity and validity
5: Sample Exemplar Quotes	Make sure the quotes are clearly connected to the parent theme	Supports representativeness
6: Balance Theme Descriptions	Consider the quality and length of the description and use of quotes	Ensures credibility in interpretation of the results
7: Illustrate Results With a Table or a Figure	Explain key results, conditions, or processes	Provides a snapshot for readers
8: Refrain From Direct Interpretation of the Results	Stick to the actual results	Stays true and close to the data
9: Summarize Themes	Provide an overview to readers	Prepares for writing up the Discussion section

CHAPTER 8: WRITING THE DISCUSSION SECTION

Step	Why do I need the step?	How will the step help my research?
1: Summarize and Interpret Key Results	Orient the reader to the major results	Provides key takeaways
2: Describe Limitations	Disclose how recruitment, study retention, participant availability, or other issues affected the study	Cautions readers to interpret the results in light of the limitations
3: Address Shifts in Positionality and Alternative Explanations	Provide possible reasons for the results	Reflects ongoing learning from the results and from field engagement
4: Compare Study Results With Those of Past Studies	Examine the results vis-à-vis the studies covered in the Introduction and Literature Review sections	Shows the contribution of this specific study to the larger field
5: Elucidate Contribution to Theory	Connect results to a larger theory, framework, or construct	Demonstrates participation in the larger conversations trending in your field
6: Articulate Transferability and Recommendations for Policy and Practice	Figure out how the results might be used in practice	Propitiates actionable or usable knowledge

CHAPTER 8: PUBLISHING YOUR WORK

Step	Why do I need the step?	How will the step help my research?
1: Convert a Project, Thesis, or Dissertation Into a Publication	Disseminate the study results	Provides a venue for others to learn about the study
2: Identify and Compare Journals in Qualitative Research	Figure out which best fits your project	Enhances the chances of getting published
3: Consider the Journal's Focus	Further align the journal to your field	Helps communicate to the most appropriate audience
4: Find Articles Related to Your Design or Analysis	Use the articles as examples for writing your manuscript	Models how to write up the study

Appendix B:
Resources for
Qualitative Researchers

QUALITATIVE RESEARCH PROGRAMS

If you are considering continued studies in qualitative research, here is a list of programs, degrees, and certificates that you can explore.

Program, degree, or certificate name	Institution
Qualitative and Mixed Methods Research Methodologies	University of Cincinnati, School of Education
Qualitative Research Methods Certificate	University of Connecticut
Research Methods and Statistics, Specialty in Qualitative Research	University of Denver, College of Education
Advanced Qualitative Methods in Conflict Studies	Peace Research Institute, Norway
Research Methods Graduate Certificate, Qualitative Research	George Mason University
Qualitative Research Methods	Georgetown University, School of Public Policy
Graduate Certificate, Qualitative Research Methods	Michigan State University
Graduate Certificate in Qualitative Research	University of Missouri, College of Education and Human Development
Qualitative Methodologies Emphasis	University of Toronto, Ontario Institute for Studies in Education
UW/QUAL Program	University of Washington, School of International Studies

(continues)

Program, degree, or certificate name	Institution
Graduate Certificate in Qualitative Research Methods	Western Michigan University, Department of Educational Leadership, Research and Technology
Doctoral minor in Qualitative Methods in Education	University of Wisconsin, School of Education
PhD in Qualitative Research and Evaluation Methodologies	University of Georgia, College of Education
Certificate in Interdisciplinary Qualitative Studies	University of Georgia
PhD, specialization in Qualitative Methods	University of Florida, College of Education
Graduate Certificate in Qualitative Research	University of Alabama
PhD in Qualitative Research	University of Cape Coast, Ghana
Qualitative Research Certificate	Purdue University
Graduate Certificate in Qualitative Research	Kent State University
Qualitative Research Graduate Certificate	Kansas State University
Graduate Certificate in Qualitative Studies	University of North Carolina
Certificate in Qualitative Research	Nova Southeastern University
Qualitative Research Graduate Certificate	University of South Florida, College of Education
Graduate Certificate in Qualitative Research in Education	University of Memphis, Department of Counseling, Educational Psychology and Research
Qualitative Research Method	University of Tennessee
Qualitative Methodology Advanced Concentration	University at Buffalo, State University of New York
Qualitative Research in Education Graduate Certificate	Georgia State, College of Education and Human Development
Certificate of Graduate Study in Qualitative Research	University of South Carolina, College of Education
Graduate Certificate in Qualitative Research in Education	Ball State University
Advanced Training in Qualitative Health Research Methodology Certificate	University of Toronto
Postgraduate Certificate in Qualitative Health Research Methods	University of Oxford

QUALITATIVE RESEARCH INSTITUTIONS

Name	Institution
Qualitative Research Program	University of Georgia, College of Education
Institute for Qualitative and Multi-Method Research	Syracuse University, School of Citizenship and Public Affairs
Institute for Social Science Research	University of Massachusetts, Amherst
Social Science Research Institute	Duke University
Center for Qualitative and Mixed Methods	RAND Corporation, California
International Institute for Qualitative Methodology	University of Alberta
Institute for Social Science Research	Arizona State University
Center for Ethnographic Research	University of California, Berkley
Qualitative Research Forum	University of Cambridge
Qualitative Research Discussion Group	Yale University
Qualitative and Interpretive Research Institute	Cornell University
Harvard Chan Qualitative Methods Student Club	Harvard University
Center for Qualitative Studies in Health and Medicine	Johns Hopkins University, Department of Health, Behavior and Society
Qualitative Applied Health Research Centre	Kings College, London
Centre for Excellence in Qualitative Health Research and Teaching	University College London
Intersectional Qualitative Research Methods Institute	University of Maryland
McGill Qualitative Health Research Group	McGill University
Qualitative Research Network	University of New Mexico, Clinical and Translational Science Center
Odum Institute for Research in Social Science	University of North Carolina
Qualitative Reasoning Group	Northwestern University
QualLab	Ohio State University
Qualitative, Evaluation and Stakeholder Engagement (Qual EASE)	University of Pittsburgh, Center for Research on Health Care
Qualitative Data Analysis Program	University of Pittsburgh, Center for Social and Urban Research

(continues)

Name	Institution
Qualitative Research Consortium	University of Missouri, College of Education and Human Development
Institute for Research in the Social Sciences	Stanford University
Center for Critical Qualitative Health Research	University of Toronto
Qualitative Services Core	University of Utah, Department of Population Health
The Interdisciplinary Qualitative Research Group	University of Washington, School of Social Work
Qualitative Research Methods Group	University of Wisconsin, School of Education
Qualitative and Mixed Methods Research Center	Rochester University Medical Center
Qualitative Research Services	Mayo Clinic, Minnesota
Center for Interpretive and Qualitative Research	Duquesne University
Centre for Qualitative Research	University of Bath, England
Qualitative Research Collaboration	University of Florida, Clinical and Translational Science Institute
Qualitative Methods Research Affinity Group	Children's Hospital of Philadelphia
Qualitative Research Core	Vanderbilt University, Center for Health Services Research
Qualitative Research Initiative	University of Illinois, Center for Social and Behavioral Science
Center for Qualitative Psychology	University of Tübingen, Germany

QUALITATIVE PROFESSIONAL ASSOCIATIONS

Several professional organizations devote themselves to qualitative research across many fields. Here are a few organizations:

American Pediatric Association, Qualitative Research Special Interest Group

American Psychological Association Division 5: Quantitative and Qualitative Methods

American Psychological Association Society for Qualitative Inquiry in Psychology

American Educational Research Association, Special Interest Group 82, Qualitative Research

Association for Qualitative Research

International Society of Qualitative Research in Sport and Exercise

Qualitative Research Consultants Association

American Sociological Association, Ethnomethodology and Conversation Analysis

---

References

Agans, R. P., Deeb-Sossa, N., & Kalsbeek, W. D. (2006). Mexican immigrants and the use of cognitive assessment techniques in questionnaire development. *Hispanic Journal of Behavioral Sciences, 28*(2), 209–230. https://doi.org/10.1177/0739986305285826

Adler, P. A., & Adler, P. (1998). Intense loyalty in organizations: A case study of college athletics. In J. Van Maanen (Ed.), *Qualitative studies of organizations* (Vol. 1, pp. 31–50). Sage.

Altheide, D. L. (1987). Reflections: Ethnographic content analysis. *Qualitative Sociology, 10,* 65–77.

American Psychological Association. (2020). *Publication manual of the American Psychological Association.* https://doi.org/10.1037/0000165-000

American Psychological Association, Science Directorate. (2015). *Tips for determining authorship credit.* https://www.apa.org/science/leadership/students/authorship-paper

Anderson, E. H., & Spencer, M. H. (2002). Cognitive representations of AIDS: A phenomenological study. *Qualitative Health Research, 12*(10), 1338–1352. https://doi.org/10.1177/1049732302238747

Angrosino, M. V. (1989). Documents of interaction: Biography, autobiography, and life history in social science perspective. *Monographs in Social Sciences No. 74,* University of Florida.

Baldwin, S. A. (2018). *Writing your psychology research paper.* American Psychological Association. https://doi.org/10.1037/0000045-000

Bandura, A. (1997). *Self-efficacy: The exercise of control.* W. H. Freeman.

Banks, J. (1998). The lives and values of researchers: Implications for educating citizens in a multicultural society. *Educational Researcher, 27*(7), 4–17. https://doi.org/10.3102/0013189X027007004

Barry, C. A., Britten, N., Barber, N., Bradley, C., & Stevenson, F. (1999). Using reflexivity to optimize teamwork in qualitative research. *Qualitative Health Research, 9*(1), 26–44. https://doi.org/10.1177/104973299129121677

Barry, W. D., & Feldman, S. (1985). *Multiple regression in practice.* SAGE Publications, Inc. https://doi.org/10.4135/9781412985208.n2

Berg, B. L. (2004). *Qualitative research methods for the social sciences* (5th ed.). Allyn & Bacon.

Bernstein, R. J. (1998). *Beyond objectivism and relativism: Science, hermeneutics, and praxis.* University of Pennsylvania Press.

Beuscher, L., & Grando, V. T. (2009). Challenges in conducting qualitative research with individuals with dementia. *Research in Gerontological Nursing, 2*(1), 6–11. https://doi.org/10.3928/19404921-20090101-04

Blumer, H. (1969). *Symbolic interactionism: Perspective and method.* Prentice Hall.

Botkin, B. A. (Ed.). (1945). *Lay my burden down: A folk history of slavery.* University of Chicago Press.

Brislin, R. (1970). Back-translation for cross-cultural research. *Journal of Cross-Cultural Psychology, 1*(3), 185–216. https://doi.org/10.1177/135910457000100301

Bryman, A. (1988). *Quantity and quality in social research.* Routledge.

Campbell, D. T. (1956). *Leadership and its effect upon the group.* Ohio State University Press.

Campbell, D. T., & Fiske, D. W. (1959). Convergent and discriminant validation by the multitrait–multimethod matrix. *Psychological Bulletin, 56*(2), 81–105. https://doi.org/10.1037/h0046016

Charmaz, K. (2011). A constructivist grounded theory analysis of losing and regaining a valued self. In F. Wertz (Ed.), *Five ways of doing qualitative analysis: Phenomenological psychology, grounded theory, discourse analysis, narrative research, and intuitive inquiry* (pp. 165–204). Guilford Press.

Chein, I. (1981). An introduction to sampling. In C. M. Judd, E. R. Smith, & L. H. Kidder (Eds.), *Research methods in social relations* (4th ed., pp. 418–441). Holt, Rinehart & Winston.

Choi, J., Kushner, K. E., Mill, J., & Lai, D. W. L. (2012). Understanding the language, the culture, and the experience: Translation in cross-cultural research. *International Journal of Qualitative Methods, 11*(5), 652–665. https://doi.org/10.1177/160940691201100508

Clandinin, D. J., & Connelly, F. M. (2000). *Narrative inquiry: Experience and story in qualitative research.* Jossey-Bass.

Clandinin, J. (Ed.). (2007). *The handbook of narrative inquiry.* Sage.

CohenMiller, A. (2018). Creating a participatory arts-based online focus group: Highlighting the transition from DocMama to Motherscholar. *The Qualitative Report, 23*(7), 1720–1735. https://doi.org/10.46743/2160-3715/2018.2895

Colaizzi, P. (1978). Psychological research as the phenomenologist views it. In R. S. Valle & M. King (Eds.), *Existential–phenomenological alternatives for psychology* (p. 6). Oxford University Press.

Connelly, F. M., & Clandinin, D. J. (1990). Stories of experience and narrative inquiry. *Educational Researcher, 19*(5), 2–14. https://doi.org/10.3102/0013189X019005002

Cornish, F., Gillespie, A., & Zittoun, T. (2014). Collaborative analysis of qualitative data. In U. Flick (Ed.), *The Sage handbook of qualitative data analysis* (pp. 79–93). Sage. https://doi.org/10.4135/9781446282243.n6

Cowan, K. (2014). Multimodal transcription of video: Examining interaction in Early Years classrooms. *Classroom Discourse, 5*(1), 6–21. https://doi.org/10.1080/19463014.2013.859846

Creswell, J. W. (2007). *Qualitative inquiry and research design: Choosing among five approaches.* Sage.

Creswell, J. W. (2008). *Educational research: Planning, conducting, and evaluating quantitative and qualitative research.* Sage.

Creswell, J. W., & Plano Clark, V. L. (2018). *Designing and conducting mixed methods research* (3rd ed.). Sage.

Cronbach, L. (1975). Beyond the two disciplines of scientific psychology. *American Psychologist, 30*(2), 116–127. https://doi.org/10.1037/h0076829

Crowe, T. (2003). Using focus groups to create culturally appropriate HIV prevention material for the deaf community. *Qualitative Social Work, 2*(3), 289–308. https://doi.org/10.1177/14733250030023005

Cruz, M. R., & Sonn, C. (2010). (De)colonizing culture in community psychology: Reflections from critical social science. *American Journal of Community Psychology, 47*(1-2), 203–214. https://doi.org/10.1007/s10464-010-9378-x

Czarniawska, B. (2004). *Narratives in social science research.* Sage.

Denzin, N. K. (1978). *The research act.* McGraw-Hill.

Denzin, N. K., & Lincoln, Y. S. (2008). *Collecting and interpreting qualitative materials* (3rd ed.). Sage.

Dewey, J. D. (1930). *Human nature and the social order.* Scribner.

Donnelly, C. M., Lowe-Strong, A., Rankin, J. P., Campbell, A., Blaney, J. M., & Gracey, J. H. (2013). A focus group study exploring gynecological cancer survivors' experiences and perceptions of participating in a RCT testing the efficacy of a home-based physical activity intervention. *Supportive Care in Cancer, 21*(6), 1697–1708. https://doi.org/10.1007/s00520-012-1716-0

Du Bois, W. E. B. (1967). *The Philadelphia Negro: A social study.* Benjamin Blom/Arno Press. (Original work published 1896)

Duveen, G. (2000). Piaget ethnographer. *Social Sciences Information, 39*(1), 79–97. https://doi.org/10.1177/053901800039001005

Esposito, F., Ornelas, J., Briozzo, E., & Arcidiacono, C. (2019). Ecology of sites of confinement: Everyday life in a detention center for illegalized non-citizens. *American Journal of Community Psychology, 63*(1-2), 190–207. https://doi.org/10.1002/ajcp.12313

Fitzgerald, C., & Withers, P. (2013). "I don't know what a proper woman means": What women with intellectual disabilities think about sex, sexuality and themselves. *British Journal of Learning Disabilities, 41*(1), 5–12. https://doi.org/10.1111/j.1468-3156.2011.00715.x

Flores, M. J., Watson, L. B., Allen, L. R., Ford, M., Serpe, C. R., Choo, P. Y., & Farrell, M. (2018). Transgender people of color's experiences of sexual objectification: Locating sexual objectification within a matrix of domination. *Journal of Counseling Psychology, 65*(3), 308–323. https://doi.org/10.1037/cou0000279

Foley, D., & Valenzuela, A. (2008). Critical ethnography: The politics of collaboration. In N. K. Denzin & Y. S. Lincoln (Eds.). *The Sage handbook of qualitative research* (3rd ed., pp. 217–234). Sage.

Foster, L. J. J., Deafenbaugh, L., & Miller, E. (2018). Group metaphor map making: Application to integrated arts-based focus groups. *Qualitative Social Work, 17*(2), 305–322. https://doi.org/10.1177/1473325016667475

Foster, M. (1994). The power to know one thing is never the power to know all things: Methodological notes on two studies of Black American teachers. In A. Gitlin (Ed.), *Power and method: Political activism and educational research* (pp. 129–146). Routledge.

Gallagher, C. A. (1999). Researching race, reproducing racism. *Review of Education, Pedagogy, and Cultural Studies, 21*(2), 165–191. https://doi.org/10.1080/1071441990210205

Geertz, C. (1973). *The interpretation of cultures: Selected essays.* Basic Books.

Gilligan, C. (1982). *In a different voice.* Harvard University Press.

Gillum, T. L. (2008). Community response and needs of African American female survivors of domestic violence. *Journal of Interpersonal Violence, 23*(1), 39–57. https://doi.org/10.1177/0886260507307650

Giorgi, A. (1985). The phenomenological psychology of learning and the verbal learning tradition. In A. Giorgi (Ed.), *Phenomenology and psychological research* (pp. 23–85). Duquesne University Press.

Glazer, B. G., & Strauss, A. L. (1967). *The discovery of grounded theory: Strategies for qualitative research.* Aldine Transaction.

Gulbas, L. E., Hausmann-Stabile, C., Szlyk, H. S., & Zayas, L. H. (2019). Evaluating the interpersonal–psychological theory of suicide among Latina adolescents using qualitative comparative analysis. *Qualitative Psychology, 6*(3), 297–311. https://doi.org/10.1037/qup0000131

Hatch, J. A. (2002). *Doing qualitative research in education settings.* State University of New York Press.

Hattan, C., & Alexander, P. A. (2021). The effects of knowledge activation training on rural middle-school students' expository text comprehension: A mixed-methods study. *Journal of Educational Psychology, 113*(5), 879–897. https://doi.org/10.1037/edu0000623

Health Insurance Portability and Accountability Act of 1996, Pub. L. 104-191, 42 U.S.C. § 300gg, 29 U.S.C §§ 1181–1183, and 42 U.S.C. §§ 1320d–1320d9. https://aspe.hhs.gov/reports/health-insurance-portability-accountability-act-1996

Henderson, D. X., Jones, J., McLeod, K., Jackson, K., Lunsford, A., & Metzger, I. (2020). A phenomenological study of racial harassment in school and emotional effects among the retrospective accounts of older Black adolescents. *The Urban Review, 52*(3), 458–481. https://doi.org/10.1007/s11256-020-00551-5

Hirsh, J. (1945). Introduction. In B. E. Botkin (Ed.), *Lay my burden down: A folk history of slavery* (pp. ix–xxv). University of Chicago Press.

Hodgins, M. J. (2017). An introduction and overview of research and knowledge translation practices in a pan-Canadian art-based health research study. *Journal of Applied Arts & Health, 8*(2), 225–239. https://doi.org/10.1386/jaah.8.2.225_1

Husserl, E. (1991). *On the phenomenology of the consciousness of internal time (1893–1917).* (J. B. Brough, Trans.). Kluwer Academic. (Original work published 1966)

Jick, T. D. (1983). Mixing qualitative and quantitative methods: Triangulation in action. In J. Van Maanen (Ed.), *Qualitative methodology* (pp. 135–148). Sage.

Katz-Buonincontro, J., Perignat, E., & Hass, R. (2020). Conflicted epistemic beliefs about teaching for creativity. *Thinking Skills & Creativity, 36*, 100651. https://doi.org/10.1016/j.tsc.2020.100651

Katz-Buonincontro, J., & Phillips, J. (2011). "Art, its creation and leadership [can be] revealing and frightening": How school leaders learn to frame and solve problems through the arts. *International Journal of Leadership in Education, 14*(3), 269–273. https://doi.org/10.1080/13603124.2011.560285

Katz-Wise, S. L., Godwin, E. G., Parsa, N., Brown, C. A., Pullen Sansfaçon, A., Goldman, R., MacNish, M., Rosal, M. C., & Austin, S. B. (2022). Using family and ecological systems approaches to conceptualize family- and community-based experiences of transgender and/or nonbinary youth from the Trans Teen and Family Narratives Project. *Psychology of Sexual Orientation and Gender Diversity, 9*(1), 21–36. https://doi.org/10.1037/sgd0000442

Kelly-Corless, L. (2020). Delving into the unknown: An experience of doing research with d/Deaf prisoners. *Qualitative Inquiry, 26*(3-4), 355–368. https://doi.org/10.1177/1077800419830133

Kita, S., van Gijn, I., & van der Hulst, H. (1997, September 17–19). *Movement phases in signs and co-speech gestures, and their transcription by human coders* [Paper]. International Gesture Workshop, Bielefeld, Germany.

Knowles, J. G., & Cole, A. L. (2008). *Handbook of the arts in qualitative research: Perspectives, methodologies, examples, and issues.* Sage.

Kohlberg, L. (1958). *The development of moral thinking and choice in the years 10 through 16* [Unpublished doctoral dissertation]. University of Chicago.

Krefting, L. (1991). Rigor in qualitative research: The assessment of trustworthiness. *American Journal of Occupational Therapy, 45*(3), 214–222. https://doi.org/10.5014/ajot.45.3.214

Krueger, R. A., & Casey, M. A. (2009). *Focus groups: A practical guide for applied research* (4th ed.). Sage.

Lazarsfeld, P. F. (1935). The art of asking WHY in marketing research: Three principles underlying the formulation of questionnaires. *National Marketing Review, 1*(1), 32–43.

LeCompte, M. D., & Preissle, J. (with Tesch, R.). (1993). *Ethnography and qualitative design in education research* (2nd ed.). Academic Press.

Levesque, J. V., Gerges, M., Wu, V. S., & Girgis, A. (2020). Chinese-Australian women with breast cancer call for culturally appropriate information and improved communication with health professionals. *Cancer Reports, 3*(2), e1218. https://doi.org/10.1002/cnr2.1218

Levinas, E. (2006). *Humanism of the other.* University of Illinois Press. (Original work published 1972)

Levitt, H. M. (2020). *Reporting qualitative research in psychology: How to meet APA Style Journal Article Reporting Standards* (rev. ed.). American Psychological Association. https://doi.org/10.1037/0000179-000

Levy, C. E., Miller, D. M., Akande, C. A., Lok, B., Marsiske, M., & Halan, S. (2019). V-Mart, a virtual reality grocery store: A focus group study of a promising intervention for mild traumatic brain injury and posttraumatic stress disorder. *American Journal of Physical Medicine & Rehabilitation, 98*(3), 191–198. https://doi.org/10.1097/PHM.0000000000001041

Liamputtong, P. (2011). *Focus group methodology: Principles and practice.* Sage. https://doi.org/10.4135/9781473957657.n10

Lincoln, Y. S., & Guba, E. G. (1985). *Naturalistic inquiry.* Sage.

Lopez, G. I., Figueroa, M., Connor, S. E., & Maliski, S. L. (2008). Translation barriers in conducting qualitative research with Spanish speakers. *Qualitative Health Research, 18*(12), 1729–1737. https://doi.org/10.1177/1049732308325857

Lopez, F. R., Wickson, F., & Hausner, V. H. (2018). Finding CreativeVoice: Applying arts-based research in the context of biodiversity conservation. *Sustainability, 10*(6), 1778. https://doi.org/10.3390/su10061778

Luttrell, W. (2010). Reflexive writing exercises. In W. Luttrell (Ed.), *Qualitative educational research: Readings in reflexive methodology and transformative practice* (pp. 469–480). Routledge.

Lykes, M. B. (2013). Participatory and action research as a transformative praxis: Responding to humanitarian crises from the margins. *American Psychologist, 68*(8), 774–783. https://doi.org/10.1037/a0034360

Malacrida, C. (2007). Reflexive journaling on emotional research topics: Ethical issues for team researchers. *Qualitative Health Research, 17*(10), 1329–1339. https://doi.org/10.1177/1049732307308948

Malmström, M., Ivarsson, B., Johansson, J., & Klefsgård, R. (2013). Long-term experiences after oesophagectomy/gastrectomy for cancer—A focus group study. *International Journal of Nursing Studies, 50*(1), 44–52. https://doi.org/10.1016/j.ijnurstu.2012.08.011

Markey, K., Tilki, M., & Taylor, G. (2019). Resigned indifference: An explanation of gaps in care for culturally and linguistically diverse patients. *Journal of Nursing Management, 27*(7), 1462–1470. https://doi.org/10.1111/jonm.12830

Martin, J., Sheeran, P., & Slade, P. (2017). "They've invited me into their world": A focus group with clinicians delivering a behaviour change intervention in a UK contraceptive service. *Psychology Health and Medicine, 22*(2), 250–254. https://doi.org/10.1080/13548506.2016.1242758

Maxwell, J. A. (2005). *Applied social research methods series: Vol. 42. Qualitative research design: An iterative approach* (2nd ed.). Sage.

McKenzie, K. B., & Scheurich, J. J. (2004). Equity traps: A useful construct for preparing principals to lead schools that are successful with racially diverse students. *Educational Administration Quarterly, 40*(5), 601–632. https://doi.org/10.1177/0013161X04268839

Mead, M. (1938). *The philosophy of the act.* University of Chicago Press.

Merleau-Ponty, M. (1998). *Phenomenology of perception.* Routledge. (Original work published 1945)

Merriam, S. B. (2009). *Qualitative research: A guide to design and implementation.* Jossey-Bass.

Merton, K., Fiske, M., & Kendall, P. (1956). *The focused interview: A manual of problems and procedures.* Free Press.

Miles, M. B., & Huberman, A. M. (1994). *Qualitative data analysis: An expanded sourcebook.* Sage.

Mills, G. E. (2000). *Action research: A guide for the teacher researcher.* Prentice Hall.

Mondada, L. (2018). Multiple temporalities of language and body in interaction: Challenges for transcribing multimodality. *Research on Language and Social Interaction, 51*(1), 85–106. https://doi.org/10.1080/08351813.2018.1413878

Morgan, D. L. (1997). *Focus groups as qualitative research* (2nd ed.). Sage. https://doi.org/10.4135/9781412984287

Morrow, S. L., & Smith, M. L. (1995). Constructions of survival and coping by women who have survived childhood sexual abuse. *Journal of Counseling Psychology, 42*(1), 24–33. https://doi.org/10.1037/0022-0167.42.1.24

Moustakas, C. (1994). *Phenomenological research methods.* Sage. https://doi.org/10.4135/9781412995658

Mulvale, G., Green, J., Miatello, A., Cassidy, A. E., & Martens, T. (2021). Finding harmony within dissonance: Engaging patients, family/caregivers and service providers in research to fundamentally restructure relationships through integrative dynamics. *Health Expectations, 24*(Suppl. 1), 147–160. https://doi.org/10.1111/hex.13063

Murdaugh, C., Russell, R. B., & Sowell, R. (2000). Using focus groups to develop a culturally sensitive videotape intervention for HIV-positive women. *Journal of Advanced Nursing, 32*(6), 1507–1513. https://doi.org/10.1046/j.1365-2648.2000.01610.x

National Science Foundation. (2021). *Broader impacts.* https://www.nsf.gov/od/oia/special/broaderimpacts/

Nicholson, L., Colyer, M., & Cooper, S. A. (2013). Recruitment to intellectual disability research: A qualitative study. *Journal of Intellectual Disability Research, 57*(7), 647–656. https://doi.org/10.1111/j.1365-2788.2012.01573.x

Noddings, N. (1984). *Caring: A feminine approach to ethics and moral education.* University of California Press.

Oliver, D. G., Serovich, J. M., & Mason, T. L. (2005). Constraints and opportunities with interview transcription: Towards reflection in qualitative research. *Social Forces, 84*(2), 1273–1289. https://doi.org/10.1353/sof.2006.0023

Patton, M. Q. (2002). *Qualitative research and evaluation methods* (3rd ed.). Sage.

Perera, C., Salamanca-Sanabria, A., Caballero-Bernal, J. Feldman, L., Hansen, M., Bird, M., Hansen, P., Dinesen, C., Wiedemann, N., & Vallières, F. (2020). No implementation without cultural adaptation: A process for culturally adapting low-intensity psychological interventions in humanitarian settings. *Conflict and Health, 14*, 46. https://doi.org/10.1186/s13031-020-00290-0

Piaget, J. (1961). The language and thought of the child. In T. Shipley (Ed.), *Classics in psychology* (pp. 994–1031). Philosophical Library. (Original work published 1923)

Polkinghorne, D. (1988). *Narrative knowing and the human sciences.* State University of New York Press.

Potter, J., & Wetherell, M. (1987). *Discourse and social psychology: Beyond attitudes and behaviour.* Sage.

Pramualratana, A., Havanon, N., & Knodel, J. (1985). Exploring the normative age at marriage in Thailand: An example from focus group research. *Journal of Marriage and the Family, 47*, 203–210.

Prosser, J., & Burke, C. (2008). Image-based educational research: Childlike perspectives. *LEARNing Landscapes, 4*(2), 257–273. https://doi.org/10.36510/learnland.v4i2.399

Pyrczak, F., & Bruce, R. R. (1992). *Writing empirical research reports: A basic guide for students of the social and behavioral sciences* (8th ed.). Routledge/Taylor & Francis.

Reissman, C. K. (2008). *Narrative methods for the human sciences.* Sage.

Rice, S. A. (Ed.). (1931). *Methods in social science.* University of Chicago.

Richardson, L. (1994). Writing: A method of inquiry. In N. K. Denzin & Y. S. Lincoln (Eds.), *Handbook of qualitative research* (pp. 516–529). Sage.

Rossman, G. B., & Rallis, S. F. (1998). *Learning in the field: An introduction to qualitative research.* Sage.

Roysircar, G., Thompson, A., & Geisinger, K. F. (2019). Trauma coping of mothers and children among poor people in Haiti: Mixed methods study of community-level research. *American Psychologist, 74*(9), 1189–1206. https://doi.org/10.1037/amp0000542

Ryle, G. (1949). *The concept of mind.* Hutchinson.

Seidman, I. (2013). *Interviewing as qualitative research: A guide for researchers in education and the social sciences* (4th ed.). Teachers College Press.

Seidman, I. (2019). *Interviewing as qualitative research: A guide for researchers in education and the social sciences* (5th ed.). Teachers College Press.

Sherriff, N., Gugglberger, L., Hall, C., & Scholes, J. (2014). "From start to finish": Practical and ethical consideration in the use of focus groups to evaluate sexual health service interventions for young people. *Qualitative Psychology, 1*(2), 92–106. https://doi.org/10.1037/qup0000014

Silverman, D., & Marvasti, A. (2008). *Doing qualitative research.* Sage.

Spradley, J. P. (1979). *The ethnographic interview.* Holt Rinehart & Winston.

Squires, A. (2008). Language barriers and qualitative nursing research: Methodological considerations. *International Nursing Review, 55*(3), 265–273. https://doi.org/10.1111/j.1466-7657.2008.00652.x

Stake, R. E. (1995). *The art of case study research.* Sage.

Stake, R. E. (2000). Case studies. In N. K. Denzin & Y. S. Lincoln (Eds.), *Handbook of qualitative research* (2nd ed., pp. 435–454). Sage.

Standing, K. (1998). Writing the voices of the less powerful: Research on lone mothers. In J. Ribbens & R. Edwards (Eds.), *Feminist dilemmas in qualitative research* (pp. 186–202). Sage.

Strauss, A., & Corbin, J. (1990). *Basics of qualitative research: Grounded theory procedures and techniques*. Sage.

Strauss, A. L. (1990). *Qualitative analysis for social scientists* (2nd ed.). Cambridge University Press.

Taylor, E. W. (2002). Using still photography in making meaning of adult educators' teaching beliefs. *Studies in the Education of Adults, 34*(2), 123–139. https://doi.org/10.1080/02660830.2002.11661466

Tisdell, E. (2008). Feminist epistemology. In L. M. Given (Ed.), *The Sage encyclopedia of qualitative research methods* (pp. 332–336). Sage.

Toolis, E. E., & Hammack, P. L. (2015). The lived experience of homeless youth: A narrative approach. *Qualitative Psychology, 2*(1), 50–68. https://doi.org/10.1037/qup0000019

Tracy, S. J. (2013). *Qualitative research methods: Collecting evidence, crafting analysis, communicating impact*. Wiley-Blackwell.

Van Maanen, J. (1982). Fieldwork on the beat. In J. Van Maanen, J. M. Dabbs, & R. R. Faulkner (Eds.), *Varieties of qualitative research* (pp. 103–151). Sage.

Van Maanen, J. (Ed.). (1998). *Qualitative studies of organizations* (Vol. 1). Sage.

van Manen, M. (1997). *Researching lived experience: Human science for an action sensitive pedagogy*. State University of New York Press.

Waller, W. (1932). *Sociology of teaching*. Wiley.

Wertz, F. J., Charmaz, K., McMullen, L. M., Josselson, R., Anderson, R., & McSpadden, E. (2011). *Five ways of doing qualitative analysis: Phenomenological psychology, grounded theory, discourse analysis, narrative research, and intuitive inquiry*. Guilford Press.

Wolcott, H. F. (1999). *Ethnography: A way of seeing*. Rowman & Littlefield.

Yin, R. K. (2003). *Case study research: Design and methods* (2nd ed.). Sage.

Yin, R. K. (2005). *Introducing the world of education: A case study reader*. Sage.

Index

About the Author

Jen Katz-Buonincontro, PhD, MFA, is a professor and associate dean of research in the School of Education at Drexel University in Philadelphia, Pennsylvania. She serves as Division 10 president for the Society for the Psychology of Aesthetics, Creativity and the Arts and was 2016 recipient of the Daniel E. Berlyne Award for Outstanding Research by an Early Career Scholar from the American Psychological Association. Helping children and adults learn to think and act in creative ways that optimize their academic and professional success is the central motivation of her research, teaching, and service. Dr. Katz-Buonincontro's research is funded by the National Science Foundation, the U.S. Department of Education, the Andrew W. Mellon Foundation, and the Windgate Foundation. She teaches research methods, creativity, and leadership development courses and welcomes collaboration with students and researchers.

About the Series Editor

Arthur M. Nezu, PhD, DHL, ABPP, is Distinguished University Professor of Psychological and Brain Sciences, professor of medicine, and professor of public health at Drexel University. He is currently editor-in-chief of *Clinical Psychology: Science and Practice*, as well as previous editor of both the *Journal of Consulting and Clinical Psychology* and *The Behavior Therapist*. He also served as an associate editor for the journals *American Psychologist* and *Archives of Scientific Psychology*. His additional editorial positions include chair of the American Psychological Association's (APA's) Council of Editors, member of the advisory committee for APA's *Publication Manual* (7th ed.), and member of the task force to revise APA's Journal Article Reporting Standards for quantitative research. His research and program development have been supported by the National Cancer Institute, the National Institute of Mental Health, the Department of Veterans Affairs, the Department of Defense, the U.S. Air Force, the Pew Charitable Trusts, and the Infinite Hero Foundation. Dr. Nezu has also served on numerous research review panels for the National Institutes of Health and was a member of APA's Board of Scientific Affairs as well as a member of the Board of Directors of both the American Board of Professional Psychology and the Society of Clinical Psychology. He is previous president of both the Association for Behavioral and Cognitive Therapies and the American Board of Behavioral and Cognitive Psychology and the recipient of numerous awards for his research and professional contributions.